D0946736

Revolutionary War: Western Response

Revolutionary War: Western Response

EDITED BY

DAVID S. SULLIVAN

AND MARTIN J. SATTLER

COLUMBIA UNIVERSITY PRESS

NEW YORK AND LONDON

The editors assume no responsibility for contributors' statements of fact or opinion. These essays were brought together to provide a balanced confrontation of diverse perspectives on a highly controversial subject. The arguments and conclusions of each author and editor are his own.

First published by the *Journal of International Affairs* as Volume XXV, Number 1, May, 1971.

Columbia University Press Paperback and book edition 1971

Library of Congress Catalog Card Number: 73-171976
ISBN: Clothbound 0-231-03564-0
Paperback 0-231-08664-4

Printed in the United States of America

Preface

Because anti-war sentiment is gathering genuinely popular momentum, some of the basic assumptions which animated our involvement in Southeast Asia will necessarily receive detailed scrutiny. As newspapers expose the duplicity which sustained and nourished the Vietnam commitment, as television talk shows dramatize the bitterness and disillusionment of returning servicemen, and as the academic community seriously reconsiders the requirements of foreign policy, the public will become increasingly conscious of what have been the motivations, options, and decisions of our military and political leaders and of the consequences of their actions. Hopefully, such an exposure will impel a public reappraisal of the cold war shibboleths held so self-righteously by many in this country, yet will not permit the nation to succumb to an orgy of simplistic and gratifying recrimination. Guided by a sense of urgency but without relying on expediency, those who undertake such a task must remain diligent and objective without sacrificing candor and, more importantly, must exhibit the determination to assess the past honestly, to appraise the present, and to prepare for the future. And if the policies and actions of those who lead this country require judicial review, then this must be faced forthrightly and without glib moralizing or facile rationalization.

Unquestionably, as the reappraisal begins, individual political and military leaders will be maligned. Stubbornly held myths will be destroyed and a search for scapegoats, war criminals, back-stabbers, etc., will be tempting. Yet if the effort is important enough to be made, then as a people,

Americans must not yield to demagoguery, rely on single-factor explanations, or condone vendettas. And if it is assumed that the nation will not descend to the anti-heroics which typified McCarthyism, then it must also be presumed that those who presently represent the political-military establishment will not contrive to restrict the public's right to know or to dismiss blandly the inhumanity of this war.

Dissent against the Vietnam policies of the United States ranges from moral outrage through practical concerns about the war's domestic effects to dissatisfaction with the war's length and disappointing results. These varying sentiments share one basic characteristic: they all express disdain for the participation, policies, or practices of the United States. However, another perspective deserves equal attention. Few Americans appreciate or consider the enemy's motivation and strategy. Thus, most neglect the distinct possibility that the nationalistic tenacity of the NLF/PRG—not the support of Hanoi, Peking, or Moscow—may have had a decisive influence on this country's failure to accomplish its objectives, however vague and mutable. Consequently, a well-balanced assessment must weigh the perspectives and strategies of both contenders.

The tendency to obscure the strategy of the NLF/PRG is abundantly evident in the terminology used by the bureaucrats and even by scholars; it reflects a conscious unwillingness to acknowledge the *sine qua non* of the conflict: the sociological dimensions and underlying political causes of the "insurgency." To classify the Vietnam war as an insurgency—in which the authority of a particular regime is challenged—rather than a revolution—in which the legitimacy of an entire social structure is contested—portrays Vietnamese history and society fatuously and selectively. This surrealistic distortion has tragically transformed a Vietnamese conflict into a Vietnamese-American war.

This anthology will offer the reader an in-depth, trenchant appraisal of these aspects of revolutionary guerrilla war. Taken together the essays provide a solid beginning for a journey toward an understanding of the revolutionary ferment and strategy rife in the Third World. And without such a journey as an integral dimension of the Vietnam critique, this country cannot avoid a future maelstrom.

MARTIN J. SATTLER

New York
June, 1971

Introduction

> ...Trying to stop a revolutionary movement by troops in the field is like using a broom to hold back a great ocean.
>
> Woodrow Wilson, Paris, 1919

This book is about the modern phenomenon of revolutionary war, also commonly referred to as "insurgency," "guerrilla war," "People's War," or "war of national liberation." Despite the enormous amount of commentary on the Indochina War, few writers have dealt systematically with the nature of revolutionary war, its dynamics, or its international repercussions. The following essays offer some important and unusual perspective on these aspects of revolutionary war, a phenomenon all too relevant to the future, especially in Latin America and Asia.

The Indochina War has been very different from past American wars for many reasons. Whatever their other misperceptions, policy-makers and military leaders have never adjusted to the special circumstances of revolutionary war. The conventional American military response to the *political* challenges of revolutionary war has mistakenly been labeled "counter-insurgency," while the sociological nature and underlying historical causes of the "insurgency" have been neglected. Thus the American strategy has wrongly employed firepower and large-scale military operations to the detriment of somewhat more rational political, social, and economic subsidiary programs of "counter-insurgency." The communists, however, have not been engaged in "insurgency"; they have been making revolution. Their revolutionary movement has successfully endured the application of tremendous military force by the world's most powerful nation.

Many critics have observed that this conventional military response to revolutionary war has been shaped and sustained by a militarized American political culture which continues to reflect the rigid psychology of the Cold War era. This political culture, perhaps best characterized by "technological anti-communism," conditions the biases and perceptions, and therefore the policy outputs, of the political system; manifests itself in a militarized foreign policy; and stimulates American interventionism around the globe.[1] Additionally, the constitutional structure of the American foreign policy-making process itself—"an invitation to conflict"—often has decidedly detrimental effects upon policy outputs and their execution. Indeed, inefficiency and conflict between and within the Legislative and Executive branches are the constitutionally established characteristics of American foreign policy-making. Foreign policy outputs also seem non-Clausewitzian: instead of military strategy being tailored to political objectives, the reverse has more usually been true, at least since 1941. Policy consensus must be built in spite of competing bureaucratic vested interests inherent in a pluralistic political system of dispersed, shared powers and responsibilities. The consequent necessity for bargaining, compromise, and "incrementalism" places a premium upon the effective communication of information within the system, but bureaucratic conflict and the Cold War ideology have a distorting effect on information transmission and perceptions of reality. Thus, the critique runs, within the environmental constraints imposed by the militarized political culture and the uncoordinated institutional structures of the foreign policy-making process, the Indochina War policy and its execution through contradictory strategies can ultimately be seen as the product of bureaucratic politics—especially interservice rivalry. Many critics conclude that broadly defined "national interests" are often adversely affected in this process; illusory ends are pursued by unjustifiable means. Beyond the failure to achieve our objectives in Indochina, the *direct* consequences of the Draconian American intervention in a revolutionary war have obviously been grossly counter-productive domestically: economic dislocation, severe political cleavages, erosion of confidence in the political system itself, increasing governmental authoritarianism, exacerbation of racial conflict, and charges of atrocities. Historically, the politics of revolutionary wars have not been confined by national boundaries but have had far-reaching effects. Expeditionary forces have more often met defeat at home than in the field.

In the first essay, Professor Eqbal Ahmad presents an interesting ideological analysis of revolutionary war, arguing that interservice rivalry and

American bureaucratic misapprehension of revolutionary war have resulted in four competing and incompatible approaches to "counter-insurgency"—each of which cancels out the others and all of which together are inadequate to crush revolution. These four approaches can be seen as clear manifestations of the militarized political culture. His analysis lays bare the inadequacies of bureaucratic information processing, the cognitive dissonance embodied in "bureaucratic truths," and the often mutually exclusive outcomes of bureaucratic politics. Ahmad's discussion of revolutionary war might be compared with a somewhat similar analysis in Sir Robert Thompson's three books and with the works of Eric Wolf.

Additionally, Ahmad analyzes some of the inevitable domestic repercussions of intervention in a revolutionary war, which his own situation perhaps exemplifies. Unfortunately, he was unable to update his discussion of these effects to include such phenomena as civilian surveillance by Army Intelligence, the tragic events of May 1970 on college campuses, the rash of bombings by the alienated Left, or the divisive 1970 Congressional campaigns. He notes some significant parallels between the Algerian War and the current Indochina War. While inquiry into the disturbing possibility of American war crimes in Indochina is a matter of legitimate public concern, Professor Ahmad's specific allegation is his own responsibility.

In the second essay, Ambassador Robert W. Komer presents an excellent historical summary of American "counter-insurgency" pacification efforts in Vietnam, focusing on some often-ignored and misunderstood constructive programs of "nation-building." He argues that despite the war's enormous political, military, economic, and psychic costs, there are some grounds for guarded optimism. Komer's interpretation of revolution in Vietnam and recent American–South Vietnamese policies affecting the villages, the historic foundation of Vietnamese society and politics, might be contrasted to the works of John T. McAlister, Jr. and Paul Mus. The conflict between the American military and civilian agencies over the strategic priority of the political, social, and economic pacification programs of "counter-insurgency" is apparent in Komer's discussion.

Certain other related factors in the American approach to the Indochina War have been widely noted: our enthnocentric failure to benefit from British or French experience with revolutionary warfare or to understand the Vietnamese environment; our failure to learn from the Moro and "Banana Wars" and from our "loss" of China in a similar revolutionary war; the necessary emphasis of "pacification" upon temporary amelioration of the rural effects of the contradictory "big unit war" (such as the "generation" by search and destroy operations of over three million refugees) rather than upon the protection and counter-mobilization of the peasantry; the failure to neutralize the crucial Viet Cong *infrastructure;* the lack of unity of command or of a political Proconsul; the operational constraints of conventional war doctrines, tactics, and training; the political, military, and economic ramifications of the oversized ARVN; etc. Furthermore, it should be clear that sovereignty, legitimacy, and democracy cannot be provided to one government by another, and that the expenditure of twice the bomb tonnage of World War II has contributed little to this effort. These factors should be forthrightly evaluated.

In the third essay, M. Jean Baechler, a colleague of Raymond Aron, delineates some of the historical lessons of French experience with revolutionary war in Indochina and Algeria. Had the U.S. taken cognizance of the military history of the French, a tragic and needless duplication of errors, including intervention itself, might have been avoided in Vietnam. Baechler skillfully employs Clausewitzian maxims in analyzing revolutionary war and French operations, concluding that the defensive strategic advantages, political and military, of a popularly-based revolutionary movement are insuperable. Perhaps his most important point is that intervention in a revolutionary war by a pluralistic, democratic nation inevitably erodes and perverts (both at home and in the client state) the very democratic principles in the name of which the war is being prosecuted.

Professor Walter W. Goldstein offers a penetrating analysis of the American political system in light of the second Indochina War, concluding pessimistically that because countervailing powers cannot be mobilized within the institutional structure of the government, the Executive's monopoly of war-making powers will impel the nation into future counter-revolutionary interventions. While Ahmad and Baechler view the warping of democratic processes as a direct result of counter-revolutionary interventions, Goldstein sees a reverse causality. He views the foreign and domestic power of the Defense Department as a pervasive cultural phenomenon. He would argue that the causes of our intervention and subsequent failure in Indochina were the organization and structure of our institutions and the militarization of "Manifest Destiny." The work of Colonel James A Donovan and General David Shoup provides supporting evidence, as do recent revelations in the news media. If, indeed, a compulsion toward global intervention in the wave of revolutionary wars forecast by many for the Third World's future is *inherent* in the American political system, then it is cause for some concern that the government has not even acknowledged the tactical lessons of present failures or designed a realistic counter-revolutionary war strategy to correct the huge disadvantages of the conventional response which continues to mire the U.S. in Vietnam.

Finally, John H. Hoagland discusses some little-known consequences of great power military aid programs in the Third World. The frequency with which American-supplied weapons inadvertently fall into the hands of revolutionaries should be noted by advocates of the application of the Nixon Doctrine. Hoagland also outlines the ill-fated development of "counter-insurgency" strategy during the New Frontier and offers some interesting speculations on the entire spectrum of future political violence from urban terrorism to revolutionary wars.

Thoughtful Americans are beginning to comprehend the vast domestic and international implications of a counter-revolutionary foreign policy, particularly its domestic costs in potential repression and in lost opportunities for social reform. Given the great inertia of a political culture nurtured by a powerful "national security" complex, given the resulting counter-revolutionary foreign policy, and given the counter-productive consequences of the execution of this foreign policy by competing bureaucracies, some critics have suggested the obsolescence of our present constitutional and institutional governmental structure. In the absence of reconstructive statesmanship to revive the countervailing powers provided for in the Constitution and to redefine our international role, critics argue that the prevailing American role as counter-revolutionary superpower in the international state system will exercise a continuing determinism upon our constitutional processes and domestic politics, increasingly warping democracy and leading toward reactionary political authoritarianism. A thorough understanding of the complex dynamics of revolutionary war could lead to the abandonment of a counter-revolutionary foreign policy or, barring that, at least to greater bureaucratic coordination and effectiveness in the execution of what may be inevitable future interventions by the United States.

David S. Sullivan

New York
June, 1971

Contents

EQBAL AHMAD

Revolutionary War and Counter-Insurgency

I. *The Nature of Revolutionary Warfare*

Occupied nations and oppressed peoples have resorted to guerrilla warfare throughout recorded history. But only in modern times has it become the acknowledged weapon of the weak, a symbol of our age registering successes no less than setbacks from China to Cuba, Malaya to Mozambique. Some 28 prolonged guerrilla insurgencies were reported by the Pentagon in 1958, 42 in 1965, and in 1969 about 50 were underway.[1] Its unprecedented popularity symbolizes the progressive severance of traditional social and economic links, the rapid erosion of authority, and a profound moral explosion among the disinherited, disenchanted masses in underdeveloped countries. It indicates the increasingly perceptible gap between the poor and the rich, between the coercive military capabilities of the rulers, and the desperate, determined resistance of the ruled. It also

[1] For 1958-1965 figures, see Samuel P. Huntington, *Political Order in Changing Societies* (New Haven, Conn.: Yale University Press, 1968), p. 4.

Eqbal Ahmad is a Fellow at the Adlai Stevenson Institute in Chicago and an editor of *Africasia*, a Paris-based journal of the Third World. Accepting full legal responsibility for this article, he is now one of the defendants in the "Kissinger kidnapping conspiracy case," and notes his inability to update his conclusion, completed in summer, 1969.

Section I is adapted from the forthcoming book, edited by Rod Aya and Norman Miller, *NATIONAL LIBERATION: REVOLUTION IN THE THIRD WORLD* (New York: Free Press, due March, 1971). Section II is adapted from Eqbal Ahmad's forthcoming book, *REACTION AND REVOLUTION IN THE THIRD WORLD* (New York: Pantheon).

constitutes man's supreme challenge to the awesome power of modern machines. Vietnam and Algeria are cases in point. Small, underdeveloped nations, they engaged two of the most advanced and murderous war machines of our time, and defeated the presumption of collective technology. Their incredible victories are lasting monuments to the power of politics and to the unconquerable will and indomitable spirit of man.

Interest in guerrilla warfare has developed rapidly in the U.S. The subject is studied with a sense of urgency in universitities no less than in military schools, by policy makers no less than by professors and journalists, for America's security and power are believed to be at stake. In general, this belief is based on two assumptions and at least one serious misconception. It assumes that the Vietnamese situation is typical, historically and politically, of other underdeveloped countries, and that American policy toward other Third World nations would be comparable to the one pursued in Vietnam. The misconception concerns the nature of revolutionary warfare.

The organizers of guerrilla warfare give prime attention, in practice no less than in theory, to the human factor. T. E. Lawrence (of Arabia) spoke of guerrilla war in terms of "the algebraic element of things, the biological element of life, and the psychological element of ideas."[2] Although Lawrence's goals were essentially military, military considerations constituted for him only one-third of the problem of organizing and sustaining guerrilla troops. Tito noted "the relative unimportance of geographical factors in the development of a rising. The basic factor is studious political work, the attitude of the mass of people and the fighting leadership —if these are present the population would fight to the last man."[3] Mao Tse-tung states "because guerrilla warfare basically derives from the masses and is supported by them, it can neither exist nor flourish if it separates itself from their sympathies and cooperation."[4] This belief in the necessity of commanding popular support governs the movement through all stages of its development, and the point is hammered into the combatants by various means including the use of popular dictums. "The populace is for the revolutionaries what water is for the fish" is the famous dictum of Mao; and the Japanese, with unparallelled honesty, called their brutal North China operations "the draining of water."

[2] T. E. Lawrence, "Guerrilla Warfare," *Encyclopaedia Britannica* (14th Edition), Vol. 10, p. 951.

[3] Vladimir Dedijer, *With Tito Through the War: Partisan Diary* (London: Hamilton, 1951), pp. 341-342.

[4] Samuel B. Griffith, Brig. Gen. USMC (ret.), translator, *Mao Tse-tung on Guerrilla Warfare* (New York: Praeger, 1961), p. 44.

"The peasant is for the revolution what air is for life," ran an Algerian dictum; and, in impotent rage, the French army tortured peasants and napalmed villages in a relentless *ratissage* that lasted more than seven years and cost about a million innocent lives. (In Vietnam the inability of the Saigon government and American troops to hold territory even during the day—which absolves them of responsibility toward the population—and greater reliance on air power, make for even less selective, if more efficient, massacre of civilians.)

The guerrilla concern with mass support is understandable even on purely military grounds. Mobility, for example, depends on the availability of food, shelter, road gangs, labor for laying mines and booby traps, messengers and stretcher bearers—services which require active and clandestine civilian cooperation right under the enemy's nose. Mobility allows the guerrillas to surprise the enemy as well as to dodge him. Good information on enemy movements and plans enables the guerrillas to choose their time and place for ambush and to escape anti-guerrilla mopping-up operations. Intelligence depends on intimate contacts with the population to the extent that it develops into a widely based rebel infrastructure which includes women, old men, and children. (The young spies who sit on trees to signal the approach of Marines and ARVN soldiers are daily casualties, and are counted as dead Vietcong. Try terrorizing a child into obedience, or a mother into sending her son to death.) Lastly, popular support is essential because the disparity of military strength rules out a clear-cut victory by the insurgents. The struggle tends to be a war of attrition in which the guerrillas' morale is their ultimate trump card, and morale cannot be sustained in isolation from one's people. History confirms the sovereignty of the human factor in revolutionary warfare.

The Algerian revolution, the least studied in this country though it comes closest to the Vietnamese situation, became a political success, although a military failure, when de Gaulle negotiated independence. The French military effort in Algeria was formidable. A total of some 800,000 troops (500,000 army regulars, 300,000 militia and police, not counting the powerful minority of a million armed French citizens hostile to the nationalists) in a population of nine million Muslims (one soldier for eleven Algerians) were tied down by a guerrilla force whose number did not exceed 35,000 regular combatants (a ratio of 23:1). In 1958 the construction of the Morice and Challe electrified fences, guarded by a military cordon across the frontier, had turned the flow of arms and men to trickles. More than two million people were moved into "regroupment centers" (a euphemism for concentration camps), and torture and napalming of villages were widely practiced. By 1961 the inside guerrillas had been reduced to some 5,000, and their ability to engage the French at will had markedly declined. But France faced a sullen Algerian population that it had conquered but could not rule. It outfought the F.L.N. but the latter continued to outadminister and "illegitimize" the French. A senior French official told me with a note of incomprehension that the "Algerians have developed a suicidal complex."

Why did the Algerian peasants risk, for seven remorseless years, their lives, the honor of their women, and the security of their paltry belongings? Nationalism alone could not explain their violent and resolute rejection of French rule. In no other colony, except Indochina, did the movement for independence take so violent a turn. And why did the peasants not respond earlier to the militants' calls to arms? The time was not "ripe," one of the historic chiefs of the Algerian revolution told me. There had been riots, demonstrations, and in 1948 what amounted to a spontaneous insurrection in Constantine. These events occur where foreign rule is resented, where acute grievances exist and institutional channels for ventilating and satisfying them are ineffective. These spontaneous and periodic disturbances as expressions of frustration over social and economic conditions are a necessary but not a sufficient condition for guerrilla revolution. Revolutionary warfare does not require simply discontent among the masses but a sense of desperation and a grim determination to end injustice and humiliation. It demands patience with prolonged suffering, and a determined conspiracy of silence and militancy.

A people can summon up that resolution only if they feel morally alienated from their rulers, when the latter's very title to authority begins to be actively rejected by the masses. As an Algerian leader asserted, "the success of a revolutionary war is predicated upon the continual and increasing moral isolation of the enemy. When it becomes total the war has been won, for the population will then fight to the last man." Later, other Algerian leaders told me that they had devoted a greater effort to fighting the French promises of eventual independence and reforms than to fighting the military. The Algerians became increasingly alienated from the French as the latter increased their military effort, which in revolutionary warfare means large-scale killing of civilians (if for no other reason than because the guerrilla is indistinguishable from other peasants), and the F.L.N. became more confident of winning not the military battles but the revolutionary war.

In the language of contemporary social science "moral isolation" will be translated as the loss of "legitimacy"—a crucial though badly defined and vastly misused term. A brief look at the nature of legitimacy, the causes of its erosion, and the problems of its re-creation is necessary to the understanding of revolutionary warfare.

Legitimacy as viewed here is not just a matter of beliefs and sentiments. It can be produced or snatched away neither by conspiracy, political conditioning nor by bargaining, neither by feats of organization nor by symbolic manipulation. It refers to that crucial and ubiquitous factor in politics which invests power with authority. Its erosion generally marks the increasing shift of citizens from obeying authority to rebelling against it. Its breakdown always heralds the arrival of revolution, for unlike rebels—who normally protest only the failures and excesses of existing authority rather than question its right to existence and who seek to redress specific wrongs rather than remodel society after a new pattern—revolutionaries challenge the existing system's very title to rule. They question the legitimacy of the entire system and seek new bases of authority in new values as well as in new political and economic arrangements.

Legitimacy comes to governments and other institutions of power when their constitutents recognize their claim to authority in some principle or source outside them, or when citizens actively and meaningfully participate in the processes of governments, i.e., when there is a maximum of self-government. Above all, legitimacy is assured to the extent that the relatonships and processes promoted by the system of power are responsive to the needs created by the system of production. In order to be legitimate, power must find an operative ideological justification—in the divine right of kings, the mandate of heaven, the sanctity of priests, or the superiority of lords; in constitutions stressing the principle of democratic consent, or in the dictatorship of the proletariat. But its functional validity comes from the concurrence of economic and social forces and needs with political institutions and relationships. The title to authority comes into question when changes in the system of production (including technology) alter the basic configuration of economic and social relationships. New knowledge, values, and classes destroy the presumptions of the old, and new ideologies offer alternatives to the existing system. As old institutions and processes inevitably begin failing to fulfill new needs and to satisfy new forces in society, the crisis of legitimacy begins. Under propitious circumstances the crisis may be resolved through reformist renovations. More often revolutions produce a new legitimacy for new systems of power.

The conditions leading to revolutions, then, are not produced by conspiracy. They are inherent in the dislocations and demands produced by rapid social change, and are predicated upon the failure of the ruling elites to respond to the needs of repudiating the old and forging new institutions and relationships. In underdeveloped countries today, the superimposition and infiltration of modern technology, industrial structures, and values are drastically altering the social and economic configurations which had, in the traditional agrarian order, assured the legitimacy of authoritative institutions and circumscribed discontent within the boundaries of religiosity and rebellion. These countries are witnessing a fundamental shift in the equation of the human condition; this change has produced a situation in which the traditional and colonial political processes and formal structures of control are at war with the conditions necessary for authority. In an excellent exposition of this development, Professor Eric Wolf has described the crisis of legitimacy as "a triple crisis generated by the demographic pressure, ecological disequilibrium, and the weakening of social ties connecting hinterland and center."[5]

The underdeveloped countries are experiencing a triple dislocation—political, social, and economic—in telescoped time. Politically, this dislocation is marked by the erosion of traditional authority, an increasing search for freedom from domination by foreigners as well as native oligarchies, by the gradual rise to political consciousness of a hitherto complacent and atomized peasantry, by their hook-up with modern, ideological counter-elites, and their growing collective expectation of justice, opportunity, and participation in national life. Socially, it is characterized by the emergence of new classes (urban workers, the crucial but underanalyzed lumpenproletariat, and a new middle class), and by cleavages of worldviews between generations and classes whereby the young and the disinherited reject the old values and agencies of socialization in favor of new ones. Among its economic manifestations is the demand not only for rapid, balanced economic development, but also for the equal distribution of wealth; and for the distribution of austerity where there is not enough wealth to distribute.

In ideological terms the triangular character of this revolution is indicated by the simultaneous appeal of nationalism, populism, and socialism—movements which were historically separate and, at first, even mutually exclusive in Europe. The overall result of this development has been a moral explosion among the masses. Men no longer accept misery, exploitation, and inequality as ordained by God. The myth of divine rulers

[5] Eric Wolf, "Peasant Problems and Revolutionary Warfare," (Paper presented to the Third Annual S.S.C., New York, September 10, 1967).

and superior races has exploded, alternative ways of ordering life and labor are increasingly understood to be available, and people believe that change in the old order of things is not only possible, but just, and therefore necessary.

The pressures for changes in political, economic, and social relationships inevitably lead to a confrontation with those whose interests lie in the maintenance of the status quo. In countries and colonies whose rulers are willing to abdicate their monopoly of power and privileges, where genuine reforms are introduced and new institutions begin to provide for a sharing of power and responsibility, the change is effected in an orderly (if not entirely peaceful) and democratic manner. Periodic and limited violence occurs, mainly in the cities, and is often exploited by aspiring politicians. But organized violence of the type used in revolutionary warfare is discouraged, rarely breaks out, and so far has not succeeded in a single country where the government made a genuine and timely effort to satisfy the grievances of the people. Nor has it succeeded in countries where the rulers have maintained some contact with the masses or where there were institutions and mechanisms through which one could hope to influence and change the existing system. It was the relative willingness to accept change, rather than the lessons in liberalism allegedly taught their subjects, that explains the comparatively orderly liquidation of the British Empire. (In independent India the communist uprising of Telingana failed not because the Indian masses have few needs, but because India's leaders, the Congress Party, and the nascent parliaments had legitimacy and held some promise for change. Similarly, India's troubles in Kashmir, Nagaland, and with the Mitzo tribes point not to the potency of community subversion, but to what happens when a government finds little moral support among a people.)

When a ruling class resists fundamental reforms (which entail reduction, if not liquidation, of its power and privileges), its confrontation with the new political forces becomes increasingly violent. A regime unwilling to satisfy popular aspirations begins to lose legitimacy. Coercion increasingly becomes its primary instrument of assuring obedience; "law and order" becomes the favorite phrase of governing groups. The revolutionary forces deliberately activate this process. By forcing the issues which augment the contradictions within the system and the divisions within the ruling class, they weaken the latter's efficacy and cohesion. By promoting activities which bring into sharp relief the parochial interests of the regime, they widen the perceptible gap between those in authority and the expectations of the collective. By their examples of defiance and challenge of the established authority, revolutionaries break the inhibitions of habitual or reflexive obedience and help transform private doubts into public actions; examples of overt resistance establish new standards of defiance and produce new alternatives and skills.[6]

Once a revolutionary movement enters the guerrilla phase, its major task is to outadminister the established authority. The main target in this bid is the village where the majority of the population lives, and where the government's presence is often chimeric and exploitative (e.g., conscription, collection of taxes). Here the chief and his council are often the main link between the people and the government. Breaking this link demands careful planning, organization, and hard work. The government is systematically eliminated from the countryside by the conversion or killing of village officials, who are then controlled and replaced by the political arm of the movement. The government is thus cut off from the population and begins, as the French graphically put it, to *légiférer dans le vide* (legislate in the void). During this phase of the movement, military confrontation is normally avoided. The embarrassed government also, at first, treats the assassinations as a police problem, while nonpayment of taxes is ascribed to administrative lags, a bad harvest, etc. The National Liberation Front is known to have gained control over 70 per cent of rural Vietnam during 1957-1962, a period in which Americans were presenting Ngo Dinh Diem as a rival of Ho Chi Minh and were going around saying, "Look, no Vietnamese army units are attacked. Therefore, there is no guerrilla threat."

Most compelling, but also most self-defeating, is the myth that terror is the basis of civilian support for guerrillas. Guerrilla warfare requires a highly committed but covert civilian support which cannot be obtained at gunpoint. No practicing revolutionary will disagree with Che Guevara's contention that "terrorism is a negative weapon which produces in no way the desired effects, which can turn a people against a given revolutionary movement, and which brings with it a loss of lives among those taking part that is much greater than the return."[7] Guerrilla resort to indiscriminate terrorism indicates lack of broad support without which the movement soon collapses. Only degenerate or defeated guerrillas are known to have risked the loss of mass support by terrorizing civilians. Widespread use of terror by some Greek guerrilla leaders "finally drove

[6] See Richard Flacks, "Social Psychological Perspectives on Legitimacy," (Paper presented at Annual Meeting of the American Psychological Association, September 1968).

[7] Ernesto Guevara, *Che Guevara on Guerrilla Warfare*, with an Introduction by Major Harries-Clichy Peterson of the U.S. Army (New York: Praeger, 1961).

over half a million of what should have been their strongest supporters into the cities and contributed to the eventual communist defeat."[8]

An outstanding feature of guerrilla training is the stress on scrupulously "correct and just" behavior toward civilians. The army code carries severe punishments for rape, robbery, and damage to property and crops. Political work, General Giap believes, is "the soul of the army," and Chinese guerrillas use army indoctrination primarily to train troops to gain the total support of the people. The guerrillas' use of terror, therefore, is sociologically and psychologically selective. It is employed partly as an instrument of subversion, and partly out of a need for survival. It strikes those who are popularly identified as the "enemy of the people"—officials, landlords, and informers. Its subversive purpose is twofold: to break the links between the government and the people; and to free the poor peasants and landless laborers who lack "tactical power" and need the revolutionary apparatus to free them from the "near complete constraint" of the oppressive power of landlords and the state bureaucracy allied to them.[9] In order to be effective, terror must be regarded by the people as an extra-governmental effort to dispense justice long overdue, and it must have the effect of freeing the local communities from the felt constraints of coercive authority.

Killing a village chief, therefore, is often a very complicated affair, and should generally prove to be unnecessary. Since most chiefs are local farmers who command legitimacy and loyalty through tradition and kinship, the revolutionaries ideally want to persuade them to join the movement. When that fails, it takes painstaking political work to convince the villagers that their chief is an "enemy of the people" and to bring about his elimination. In the early years of the Algerian revolution it took the F.L.N. from two months to a year to kill a popular but quisling village chief without incurring the liability of the village or tribal hostility, and that was an anti-colonial war. Therefore, it is amazing to learn that in Vietnam about 13,000 local officials were killed between 1957 and 1961. The number seems unusually large for a country which then had a total of some 14,000 village units; and the time seems too short for so many assassinations at the village level. Professor Bernard Fall gives a simple explanation: these chiefs, as appointees of Diem, had little legitimacy compared with the Vietminh cadres who had liberated the country from France and whom these new chiefs had replaced. Furthermore, these

[8] Peter Paret and John Shy, *Guerrillas in the 1960's* (New York: Praeger, 1962), p. 34.

[9] Eric Wolf, *op. cit.*

officials got involved, along with the American-equipped and trained ARVN, in the sordid business of restoring the landlords who had fled the country during the war. (A *de facto* land reform was achieved under the Vietminh.) These absentee aristocrats even demanded eight years' worth of back rent covering the period from 1945 to 1954. Before the war, the rent had been 50 per cent of the yield; the peasant was thus required to pay 400 per cent of his produce and to surrender his rights to the land. The Vietcong had no problem preparing the peasants to accept the killing of these officials.

The population must seem at least neutral to escape full enemy treatment by the incumbents. Rebel troops and officials do not arrive at night from "somewhere in the mountains;" they are present during the day, too, and often lead the show of obedience to the government. At night, the loyal peasant turns into a guerrilla and all know him as such. The security of the movement depends on secrecy. One renegade can destroy a whole network in the area by informing the enemy who invariably tortures him to get the names of others. Torture is a nightmare to guerrillas; therefore, they display a deep fear of, and a brutal intolerance toward, informants. To ensure that the popular conspiracy of silence develops no seams, exemplary punishments are given to those suspected of having informed the enemy.

Second-degree terror, which normally does not result in killing, is used to sabotage the government's belated effort to gain popular support and thus to perpetuate its isolation from the people. Government school teachers and health workers are favorite targets of kidnapping and indoctrination. In June, 1962, a South Vietnamese observer at the U.N. informed UNESCO that the Vietcong had kidnapped more than 1,200 teachers and that the government's malaria eradication campaign collapsed after 22 health officers had been killed and 60 kidnapped. Guerrilla sabotage normally guards against causing too much hardship on the population and long-range damage to the economy. Industry and even foreign-owned plantations are spared if they pay their "taxes" to the liberation front. And they normally do so when the government is unable to protect them. (In Vietnam the large European rubber plantations, Michelin, SIPH, and Terres Rouges resisted for a while, but started paying taxes to the NLF after their French supervisors were kidnapped. During 1966-1968, however, these plantations were severely damaged by American bombings and artillery fire.) Guerrilla sabotage is also selective, and it aims at maximum psychological effect.

The success of a movement in acquiring legitimacy, support for its programs, and participation in its parallel hierarchies depends on a number of factors. A coherent, consistent, and functioning ideology appropriate to its cultural, political, and economic environment appears to be important for success in protracted conflict between protagonists of unequal strength; it is particularly crucial in assuring a movement's continued legitimacy and the unity of its leadership after the armed phase of the struggle is over and the task of consolidation begins.

The structure, values, and leadership style of a revolution must not only promise a new vision of society, but also, at the same time, be congruent with the old culture. "Historical progression is inseparable from cultural roots" says Carlos Fuentes in explaining the appeals of the Zapatista revolution among:

> . . . campesinos, people from the field who did not in the larger sense of the term, feel culturally deprived but were conscious that a social and political opportunity was given them to realize, in actuality, the latent promises of their local culture.
> Only this profoundly civilized self-awareness can explain, first, the apparently natural talents the Zapatistas applied to guerrilla warfare in their campaign against General Juvencio Robles and Huerta's Federal Army. Zapata, the so-called "Attila of the South" was the first of the line of strategists–Castro, Guevara, the FLN fighters in Algeria, Giap in Vietnam–that have made of the guerrilla the natural defensive arm of a locally based culture. . . .[10]

Successful parallel hierarchies, therefore, are generally based on extant local patterns and experiences—a phenomenon notable in the Mexican, Russian, Chinese, Vietnamese, and Algerian revolutions.[11] Even more importantly, the symbols of revolution and styles of leadership derive heavily from the local culture and constitute the creative links between the old and the new, between the mystical and the rational bases of legitimacy.

But unlike the formal constitutions and administrative structures of most underdeveloped countries, such patterns are not the outcome of contrived, professional designing. They result from a profound and intense interaction between leaders and followers which often constitutes a greater learning experience for the urban-trained leaders than their rural comrades. Only a relationship of mutuality, identification, and co-perfor-

[10] Carlos Fuentes, "Zapata's Revolution," *The New York Review of Books,* Vol. XII, No. 3 (March 13, 1969), pp. 5-12.

[11] See for example: Sir John Maynard, *The Russian Peasant and Other Studies* (New York: Collier Books, 1962); Stuart R. Schram, *The Political Thought of Mao Tse-tung* (New York: Praeger, 1963); Paul Mus, *Vietnam: Sociologie d'Une Guerre* (Paris: Editions du Seuil, 1952).

mance between leaders and the masses can release the creative energies necessary for the constant improvisations and steady flow of new leaders (their attrition rate being very high) so crucial in revolutionary warfare. Personal background and class origins of leaders seem to be important factors in facilitating this development; the narrower the original social and cultural gaps between them and the populace, the more likely they are to create meaningful bases for authoritative leadership within a revolutionary setting. The majority of Algerian, Chinese, and Vietnamese revolutionary leaders are known to have a rural family background, and few were trained at western universities. Frequently a relationship of mutuality and identification between city-trained revolutionaries and the rural masses develops when the repressive measures of the government drive the former to seek safety in the rural areas, to communicate and live with peasants, not as proselytizing outsiders but as suffering fellow men. In the process, the leaders learn the realities of the peasant economy, social life, and the meaning and power of rural myths, symbols, and rituals; and the peasants begin to understand that their private and communal problems have wider public and political connections.

Congruence, however, does not imply absence of institutional or ideological innovation, nor even conformity to traditional structures and values. A revolution must necessarily destroy and replace the anachronistic traditional structures and values. As an organized, sustained, and largely clandestine struggle aimed at the destruction of the existing power relationships, revolutionary warfare itself represents a break from the rebellions of the past. It creates an environment in which the rural people themselves accept and introduce innovations which transform their communities; these often include innovations whose imposition by nonlegitimate rulers they had previously resisted. Eric Wolf has succinctly described the significance of this fact:

> Such a self-made social structure speeds learning. By removing the constraints of the inherited order, it releases the manifold contradictions hitherto held in check—the opposition of old and young, men and women, rich and poor—and directs the energies so freed into new organizational channels. It is this, above all, which makes revolution irreversible. It also speeds the rise of leaders from the peasantry itself, thus providing new channels of mobility not contained in the old system, and intensifying the fusion between peasantry and leadership which sparked the revolutionary effort.[12]

[12] Eric Wolf, *op. cit.* For examples of these revolutionary changes see: Frantz Fanon, *Dying Colonialism* (New York: Grove Press, 1967); Pierre Bourdieu and Abdel

Finally, there are the well-known "rational" factors, involving the promise and performance of programs, elites, and institutions, which go into the making of legitimacy: the success of a movement's program in creating common interests and collective goals (as against serving parochial interests); the actual functioning of revolutionary institutions, and the extent to which they remain accountable to the population and permit rapid recruitment and elevation of the young seeking a new identity and role in society; and the integrity of leaders, their ability to practice and promote the principles proclaimed by the revolution and cherished by the people, and their success in realizing, at least partially in the present, the popular dreams of integrated, participatory, and self-managing communities. Since the superior resources of the incumbents make coercion a poor basis of power for revolution, revolutionary movements often represent maximization of the positive basis for legitimacy. The most successful guerrilla movements, therefore, evince deep respect for local autonomy, self-management, rapid social mobility, egalitarianism, and accountability of leaders and cadres to the populace.

It is difficult to say at what point the moral isolation of an incumbent government becomes total and irreversible, so that no amount of promises and reforms would restore the lost confidence and reduce the people's resistance. Neither collective cynicism nor a people's will to fight can be measured accurately. In Algeria, at least, the point seems to have been reached when the French were reduced to the torture and killing of civilians and to *regroupement* of the population. Many Algerian leaders believe that their revolution became irreversible at the moment of France's greatest military victory—General Massu's conquest of the Casbah (the Muslim section of Algiers was reduced to rubble during 1957-1958). France could no longer expect the confidence, much less the loyalty, of a people it was destroying indiscriminately, albeit unwillingly and despite itself.

The desertion of the intellectuals and moderates often signals, not so much the irreversibility of a revolutionary war, but its take-off. Somewhat alienated from their culture, westernized and city-centered, they distrust the peasants, but desire an improvement of their condition. When an armed revolution breaks out, they are likely to play in the middle, hoping to get some reforms under way by using the armed threat as a counter

Malek Sayad, *Le Deracinement: La Crise de L'Agriculture Traditionnelle en Algérie* (Paris: Les Editions de Minuit, 1964); William Hinton, *Fanshen: A Documentary of Revolution in a Chinese Village* (New York: Vintage Books, 1966); and John Womack, *Zapata and the Mexican Revolution* (New York: Knopf, 1969).

for bargaining. These *attentistes* begin to seek exile or to defect to the rebels after the failure of the regime and the success of the revolution become imminent.

Although not a legitimitizing factor, external help has great psychological and diplomatic value for a revolutionary movement. In a war of attrition, there can be no decisive victory over a strong foreign enemy. At best, one hopes to inflict heavy losses, exhaust it, and, through international pressure, force it to negotiate—not the status quo, but withdrawal. External help is important in internationalizing guerrilla demands, and keeps alive the hope of liberation. When a revolutionary army loses an ally, it loses not so much military support; it loses hope. When the world is watching and when the fear of diplomatic sanctions and the threat of a widened war are absent, a foreign power caught in counter-guerrilla operations is likely to make the final and the only move that is likely to "win" the war—start committing genocide.

Thus, the assumption that a guerrilla force, like a conventional army, can be controlled and commanded by a foreign or externally based government ignores the organizational, psychological, and political facts of revolutionary warfare. The distrust of the "home-based" guerrillas even for their own government-in-exile cannot be overstated. The resourceful and tough "interior" leaders and cadres who face the enemy daily, collect taxes, administer, make promises, and give hopes to the population are not easily controlled from abroad and make suspicious, exacting, and hard-to-please allies. Clandestineness does not permit the use of conventional channels of communication and authority. Therefore, zone commanders and political commissars are, for the most part, monarchs of what they survey. Tested in war, seasoned in politics, accustomed to command and to quick decisions, these soldier-politicians have their own constituents, their dreams of power and community, and their commitment to expressed goals. As a group, they are joined together by shared experiences, by a common mood which is defiant and insular, by a shared suspicion of "politicians and diplomats over there" selling them out, and by a collective will to defy a settlement that is not of their making.

Summary. Studies in the field of revolutionary wars and my personal observation of the Algerian struggle lead to conclusions which may be summarized as follows: (1) Revolutionaries consider mass support the primary condition for their success; winning and maintaining popular support remains their central objective throughout the struggle. (2) The requirements of guerrilla war, as well as the history of its failures and successes, confirm the primacy of political factors in such a conflict. (3) Popular support for the guerrillas is predicated upon the moral alienation of the masses from the existing government. The revolutionaries' chief aim is to activate and perpetuate the moral isolation of the enemy regime until such isolation has become total and irreversible. (4) The conditions leading to revolutionary wars are not created by conspiracy. They are partly inherent in a situation of rapid social change, but the outbreak normally results mainly from the failure of a ruling elite to respond to the challenge of modernization. (5) A revolutionary guerrilla movement concentrates on "outadministering," not on "outfighting" the enemy. This is a constructive and not simply a destructive undertaking. (6) The use of terror by guerrillas is highly selective; it does not constitute the reason for the favorable reaction of the masses to their cause. (7) The external sanctuary has greater psychological and diplomatic value, rather than military or political value, to the guerrillas.

II. *The Nature of Counter-Insurgency*

The proponents of counter-insurgency have been the chief commentators and sources of information on the theory and practice of revolutionary warfare. As a result, the biases and prejudices of incumbents are built into the structure, images, and language of contemporary western, especially American, literature on this subject. We have come to accept ideologically contrived concepts and words as objective terms descriptive of reality.

One could take innumerable examples—terrorism, subversion, pacification, urbanization, protective reaction, defensive interdiction, etc.—and analyze the realities behind these words and phrases. The term counter-insurgency is itself an excellent example. Like all counter-revolutionary coinages it is value-laden and misleading. In fact, counter-insurgency is not at all directed against insurgency, which is defined as "a revolt against a government, not reaching the proportions of an organized revolution; and not recognized as belligerency."[13] It would be inappropriate to describe the Vietnamese and Laotian revolutions as insurgencies, or the fateful American invasion of Indochina as an exercise in counter-insurgency. In fact, the Congress and the country would be in an uproar if the government claimed that U.S. counter-insurgency capabilities were avail-

[13] *Webster's Collegiate Dictionary* Fifth Ed. (Springfield, Mass.: G & C Merriam Co., 1947). *Webster's Third New International Dictionary* (1961) gives a similar definition: "a condition of revolt against a recognized government that does not reach the proportion of an organized revolutionary government and is not recognized as belligerency."

able to its clients for putting down "revolts not reaching the proportions of an organized revolution." The opposite is true: counter-insurgency involves a multifaceted assault against organized revolutions. This euphemism for counter-revolution is neither a product of accident, nor of ignorance. It serves to conceal the reality of a foreign policy dedicated to combating revolutions abroad and helps to relegate revolutionaries to the status of outlaws. The reduction of a revolution to mere insurgency also constitutes an *a priori* denial of its legitimacy. In this article, counter-insurgency and counter-revolution are, therefore, used interchangeably.

Analytically, counter-insurgency may be discussed in terms of two primary approaches—the conventional-establishment and the liberal-reformist—and two ancillary approaches—the punitive-militarist and the technological-attritive. These latter are termed ancillary because they develop logically from involvement in counter-revolution, and from the interplay between conventional and liberal institutions and the individuals involved in it. These approaches, though identifiable in terms of the intensity and scope of their application at given times and in terms of the agencies and individuals who favor them, are operationally integrated in the "field."

It must be stressed that the theory and the practice of counter-insurgency, although monolithic in their goal of suppressing revolutions, reflect the pluralism of the western societies to which most of their practitioners and all of their theoreticians belong. For example, prominent among the partisans of pacification in its purest form have been CIA, AID, State Department, and some White House officials. The Chiefs of Staff and senior Army officers generally favor conventional deployments. The Air Force also wants its share of action and does offer the "mobility" so highly prized by the counter-insurgency experts, and the "air-support" so craved by the embattled soldiers. The Navy can hardly be left out; it must perfect its amphibious capabilities and also deserves a role in "softening" the coastal areas. Furthermore, experts differ passionately on specific details ("fix" and destroy or "search" and destroy) concerning targets, areas of pacification, methods of encirclement and interdiction, techniques of cadre training, etc.

In a pluralistic, bargaining political culture there is an institutionalized compulsion for compromise. There is something for everyone within a defined boundary, and, given a consensus on broad objectives, there is bound to be give and take. The actual strategy and tactics thus reflect a compromise such that no one blueprint is applied in its original, unadulterated form. This contributes to the most fateful phenomenon of counter-revolutionary involvement. Groups and individuals continue to feel that their particular prescriptions were never administered in full dosage and at the right intervals. They evince a tendency toward self-justification, a craving for continuing and improving their blueprints of success. As severe critics of specific "mistakes," "blunders," or "miscalculations" they seldom cease to see "light at the end of the tunnel."

We might view the conventional-establishment approach as constituting the common denominator of the assumptions and objectives shared by all incumbents; viz., a negative posture toward revolutions, a conspiratorial view of their origins, managerial attitudes toward them as a problem, and a technocratic-military approach to their suppression. In strategy and tactics, the conventional-establishment approach denotes a preference for conventional ground and air operations requiring large deployments of troops, search-and-destroy "missions" (also called "mop-up operations"), the tactics of "encirclement" and "attrition" which involve on the one hand the establishment of large military fortifications (bases, enclaves) connected by "mobile" battalions (which in Vietnam have come to mean helicopter-borne troops and air cavalries); and on the other hand, the massive displacement of a civilian population and the creation of free-fire zones.[14] The conventionalists also evince deep longings for set-piece battles, and help multiply the political and institutional pressures toward forcing, surprising, or luring the guerrillas into conventional show-downs. The results are massive and sustained aerial bombardment (e.g., North Vietnam) or invasion of enemy "sanctuaries" across the frontiers of conflict (e.g., Cambodia and Laos), and the tactic of offering an occasional bait in the hope of luring the enemy to a concentrated attack (e.g., Dien Bien Phu, Khe Sanh).

The strength of the conventional-establishment's strategy and tactics derives from the fact that it has an enormous attraction for senior officers of conventional armed forces. This approach was first associated in Algeria with General Cherrière, and in Vietnam with General Westmoreland. Being rich in tradition, it yields to multiple variations and every strong general gets the opportunity to introduce his preferred variant in a protracted intervention. While of considerable interest to competing commanders and their cliques, these variations have little theoretical im-

[14] See Jonathan Schell, *The Village of Ben Suc* (New York: Vintage Books, 1967); and by the same author, *The Military Half* (New York: Vintage Books, 1968); and Yves Courrière, *Les Fils de la Toussaint* (Paris: Fayard, 1968), Chapter 4.

portance, and no significance whatsoever for the people and culture under assault.

If the conventional-establishment attitudes constitute the lowest common denominator of counter-revolution, the liberal-reformists comprise the chief exponents of its doctrine, and the most sophisticated programmers of its practice. They provide the core of the policies associated with counter-insurgency: the creation of counter-guerrilla guerrillas (special forces), and the stress on irregular tactics, the unity of civilian and military roles, maximum use of mercenaries, psychological warfare, counter-terror, and, above all, pacification. The term liberal-reformist reflects the expressed goals as well as the political background of individuals involved in articulating and practicing this form of counter-revolution. The rhetoric which defines its goals is reformist and liberal. Freedom, progress, development, democracy, reforms, participation, and self-determination are its favorite working words. Generally, its theorists, of whom a majority come from France and the U.S.A., have been men of impeccable liberal credentials.

In the U.S., among its most prominent exponents are many of Kennedy's New Frontier men, and well-known liberal university professors. In France, the liberal-reformists include such eminent politicians as Jacques Soustelle and Robert Lacoste. In the army its exponents were reputedly the most progressive commanders who had fought in the Resistance against Nazi occupation or with the Free French Army. Humiliated by defeat in Indochina, they proceeded with determination to practice *pacification* in Algeria. Frustrated by failures there, these soldier-reformers increasingly meddled in politics. They helped destroy the Fourth Republic, rebelled against the Fifth, became accomplices of the European *Ultras*, whom they had once openly detested and from whom they had been promising to deliver the Algerians, founded the fascistic O.A.S., and ended up mercilessly massacring the natives whose freedom they had claimed to protect.

The punitive-militarist style is a product of the liberal-reformist doctrine of counter-insurgency; but it invariably acquires a life of its own. It entails irregular tactics, small-unit deployment, efficiently and relentlessly executed punitive measures against civilians suspected of aiding guerrillas, systematic use of torture, murder of prisoners, and the institution of total control over the population. At the same time the rhetoric of pacification demands that the soldiers treat the friendly and neutral population with kindness and consideration. In practice, however, distinguishing between friendly and hostile villagers is impossible. Wary soldiers in an alien environment strewn with booby-traps can only perceive all civilians as being hostile, admit the fact, act accordingly, and meet their ordered or understood quota of body-counts. (It should be recalled that after the massacre of My Lai, General Westmoreland communicated his congratulations to Company C for its body-count of 129.)[15] They make few pretenses about winning hearts and minds, although in deference to the principles of pacification, candy is sometimes distributed, music is played, and food and first-aid is provided to the survivors, especially after a hard strike.

In Algeria the punitive-militarist style was known as *style-para* in reference to the paratroopers of General Massu whose exploits included the "winning" of the hair-raising Battle of Algiers. In Vietnam it is more generalized although it appears particularly popular with the U.S. Special Forces and the mercenaries recruited by them, the Koreans, and the ARVN ranger battalions. The main virtue of this style lies in the fact that, unlike the massive "mop-ups" and clinically impersonal bombings entailed in conventional operations, it produces somewhat personalized massacres like that of My Lai which at least give the victims no less than the killers a sense of human contact. It also produces some public understanding of the war crimes which counter-revolutionary interventions often entail.[16]

Increasing reliance on technological-attritive methods marks the shift of counter-revolutionary foreign intervention in a genocidal direction. When a revolutionary war has been definitively lost—when the moral isolation and illegitimacy of the client regime becomes total and perceptibly irreversible, when even a prolonged and massive foreign intervention fails to break the "enemy's" will to resist but produces widespread anti-war sentiments at home, when draftees become restive and resistant, when the protracted war becomes bad for business and begins to contribute to the dual pressures of inflation and recession—then a great power caught in counter-revolutionary operations is left with only two alternatives. One is to negotiate withdrawal as de Gaulle did in Algeria. The other is to continue the war and subsequently to create a quasi-permanent occupation of the belligerent country, at a cost acceptable to the people at home, but costly to the "insurgents" abroad. That is the choice which defines President Nixon's policy of Vietnamization. A "semantic hoax,"

[15] Seymour Hersh, "My Lai 4," *Harper's* (May 1970), p. 72.

[16] See Telford Taylor, *Nuremberg and Vietnam: An American Tragedy* (Chicago: Quadrangle Books, 1970). See a review of this important study by Richard A. Falk in *The New York Times Book Review* (December 27, 1970), pp. 4, 14. Clergy and Laymen Concerned About Vietnam, *In the Name of America* (Annandale, Virginia: The Turnpike Press, Inc., 1968).

as Senator Harold E. Hughes described it, Vietnamization is a euphemism for the further mechanization of the war, for the application of the doctrine of permanent counter-insurgency. It is also, as Senator McGovern has stated, a manipulative move to "tranquilize the conscience of America while our government wages a war by proxy" and "perpetuates a corrupt and unrepresentative government."[17]

Sir Robert Thompson, a trusted adviser of Mr. Nixon's and a renowned expert on counter-insurgency, is one of the architects of Vietnamization, which he describes as a "long-haul, low-cost" strategy. His optimistic evaluation of Vietnamization was cited in the President's policy statement as proof of its success.[18] It is worth noting a few of the considerations which went into the making of the Vietnamization policy. First, Sir Robert warns that "a greater impact is made in a democratic society by the coffins coming home, and by higher taxes;" second, that it "will certainly take ten to fifteen years" to achieve the desired goal, i.e., a politically stable, non-communist, independent state of South Vietnam. Hence, he advises that in order to maintain public acceptance of a protracted involvement, one must show some progress: "As soon as progress is visible, even though success may still be many years away, time ceases to be such an important factor. There will be few indeed who are not then prepared to take the extra time required for victory." Third, Sir Robert thinks that "there is nothing new about the horror and tragedy of the Vietnam war except that it has been exposed to the camera and brought into the sitting room." He notes that ". . . running insurgency sores in some Latin American countries . . . have made very little impact outside the area of conflict."[19]

[17] *The New York Times*, February 8, 1970.

[18] For an earlier, more impassioned, intelligent, but also more contradiction-ridden version of this strategy, see William R. Corson, *The Betrayal* (New York: Norton, 1968), Chapter 12, pp. 262-290. Corson is an intellectual and a politicized Marine Corps Lieutenant Colonel, now retired. His conversion to pacification and subsequent anger over the "sabotage" of the "other war" by the institutions and political processes at home resemble those of the French *officier-administrateur* of *La Guerre Révolutionnaire*. He deserves special attention as a prototype of the military officers who become committed to the liberal-reformist view of counter-insurgency.

[19] Sir Robert Thompson, *No Exit From Vietnam* (New York: David McKay Co., 1970), pp. 61, 125, 163-164, 8, 169. See pp. 116 and 197 for his definition of victory. President Nixon quoted Thompson's evaluation in his televised speech of December 15, 1969. A year later (December 2, 1970) *The New York Times* reported Sir Robert as giving a "gloomy" report to President Nixon following his latest "secret mission" to evaluate the success of Vietnamization. There was a denial from the White House that the "over-all thrust of the story which leads to the impression that the pacification and Vietnamization programs are not doing well is an incorrect impression." But the White House Press Secretary refused to discuss the contents of the report "because it was secret." (*The New York Times*, December 4, 1970).

Making the war domestically acceptable thus involves turning it into a "forgotten war" (Laos as the model) by relegating it to the back pages of the newspapers, and by keeping it a maximum distance from television cameras. It entails stimulating false illusions of progress. Above all, it demands lowering the monetary costs and American casualties. The one requires reduction in the size of the expensive American manpower deployment; the other dictates avoidance of active fighting by U.S. ground forces. Both help to maintain the illusion of progress and to keep the public quiet. As Sir Robert says, "In this way the whole cost of the war, in every sense, could be reduced to a level which would be acceptable to the majority in the U.S., without proving to be an excessive drain on her manpower, money or emotions."[20]

At the same time victory requires that the war remain costly to the enemy. Their strength must be sapped, political "infrastructure" destroyed, morale undermined, and resources and bases depleted. It should be underscored that the latter is identified by Sir Robert as being "not outside the country" and not in "jungles and swamps," but in "populated areas . . . under insurgent control" and even those "areas still ostensibly under government control."[21] He recommends a return to the techniques of counter-insurgency which he successfully practiced in Malaya and which he has been prescribing as an adviser on Vietnam for more than a decade, with the conviction, of course, that they were never fully implemented. These include: inducing the Saigon regime to act in accordance with the law, without however preventing it from passing emergency laws; improving civil and military administration; defining the central government's and villages' responsibilities and obligations; selecting priority areas for pacification, and mounting fix-and-destroy ("fix," not "search," insists Sir Robert) operations in the areas outside the selected "ring." Finally: "Offensive operations into contested and enemy held areas will still be necessary, for which reason the securely held areas should be limited to allow for an adequate reserve of forces for such operations."[22] Obviously, if the policy of defeating the NLF while minimizing American costs and casualties is to succeed, then the Saigon government must progressively take over the task of governing and fighting. If the Saigon regime does not or cannot do so, then the U.S., if unwilling to

It is to be noted that the earlier but optimistic "secret" report was published as the concluding part of *No Exit From Vietnam* (pp. 208 ff.).

[20] *Ibid.*, p. 199.

[21] *Ibid.*, p. 34.

[22] *Ibid.*, p. 198.

negotiate withdrawal, has only one course of action: maximum replacement of men with machines and cost-effective offensive operations in the areas Sir Robert defines as enemy bases.

Sir Robert's and others' administrative prescriptions are irrelevant, for in a country which has been fighting a long and bitter war of national liberation no amount of managerial manipulation by foreign forces can equip *their* native "elite" with even a semblance of legitimacy, i.e., with the title to govern. This is especially true when that elite carries the stigma of having been the historic traitor to the nation, of having actively collaborated with colonial France, and now, of sanctioning the systematic destruction, by the succeeding foreign power, of a people and a country it claims to govern.[23] Hence, notwithstanding the counter-insurgents' recommendations, and their deep faith in the power of borrowed, bureaucratic, "cost-effective innovations," Vietnamization cannot mean that the Saigon government will take over the war and become viable even in "ten to fifteen years" as Sir Robert optimistically surmised.[24]

[23] Typically, counter-revolutionary scholars and U.S. government publications distort the history of Vietnam, or suppress critical information. Very little biographical information is available in English on Thieu, Ky, and Khiem, all of whom fought on the side of France during Vietnam's War of Independence (1945-1954). Since these facts are not generally known, it is worth mentioning a few: (1) *Thieu:* Graduated from Dalat Military Academy in 1948; participated in at least the following major French military operations against Vietnamese nationalists: Operation Occident—1949; Operation Hung Yen—1952 (this involved a notorious massacre); Operation Atlantic in Phou Yen. (2) *Khiem:* Enlisted with the French in 1947; staff officer of Secteur 2; commanded Operation Nettoyage ("clean-up") west of Hué; 1954-55, Chief of Staff, V Military Corps area. (3) *Ky:* Born in Son Tay where U.S. forces recently landed to "rescue" prisoners; enlisted with the French 1951; attended Reserve Officers School in Nam Dinh 1952 and Aviation School in Avord, France, 1954.

A reminder is necessary that the above operations and names, being more recent and more costly to the people at large, must be more poignantly remembered by the Vietnamese than are Bunker Hill or Valley Forge by the Americans. To expect any self-respecting Vietnamese to cooperate with or trust a government led by such men is like expecting George Washington and his colleagues to participate in a government led by Benedict Arnold and the commanders of the Hessian and British regiments.

[24] "Innovation" is a favorite word with the second-ranking counter-insurgency experts whose works I have generally ignored lest I be accused of selecting the weaker examples of counter-insurgency theory. However, I should note that with the exception of new machines and computers, bigger bombers, and a whole range of hitherto unknown killing and detection devices, there is nothing "innovative" about the American counter-insurgency effort. With the exception of the computerized HES (Hamlet Evaluation System), there is not one managerial innovation, one pacification gimmick in Vietnam—Agroville, New Life Hamlet, "Rev-Dev," Combined Campaign Plan, CORDS, Project Take-off, *Chieu Hoi*, *Phung Hoang*, APC, the "New Model Pac," etc.—that was not previously conceived and applied by the French in Indochina and/or Algeria or by the British in Malaya. Of course, the French initials were different. A reminder is needed that the one "innovation"—the HES—informed us of pacification's dramatic success ("relatively secure" hamlets grew by

Under the impact of the massive American military presence and bomb-induced "urbanization" (in Laos the "strategic movement of the people"), the Saigon regime is now in a worse predicament, although a "residual" American force equipped with the will and capacity to protect it can keep the regime in power indefinitely. A third of South Vietnam's people are estimated to be refugees (so are 25 per cent of the Laotians, and more than a million Cambodians) due almost entirely to the "air-support" provided by the U.S. The Senate Judiciary Subcommittee on Refugees headed by Senator Edward Kennedy has reported on how the pacification agencies and the Saigon government collaborate to keep the figures down, and "solve" the refugee problem by "reclassifying the refugees out of existence." The report shows how "under the banner of 'Vietnamization' a plethora of new terms and slogans have been created to describe, and hide, old problems and unchanged programs;" and how the "accelerated pacification" machinery (including the computerized HES) works to create illusions of "successes" in refugee resettlement while "new refugees continue to be generated daily, and old refugees remain where they have been for the past several years."[25]

I have mentioned the refugees rather than the dead because this "urbanized" mass, though classified out of existence, is still a reality; it makes the cities as hopeless for the incumbent regime as the rural areas. Students, workers, and Buddhists have recently risked severe repression to raise their voices in opposition. Don Luce, one of the few Americans who knows the Vietnamese language and culture and who led a group of Congressmen to the tiger cages of Con Son, reported in a television interview (recorded on November 12) that in the previous two months nearly 150,000 persons had been arrested; and that torture is widespread. Early in December, 1970, the city of Qui Nhon had an unprecedented anti-U.S. riot and massive demonstrations which then spread to Saigon in the form of widespread sabotage. Informed sources in Paris indicate that Saigon's shrewdest politicians are quietly currying favor with the Provisional Revolutionary Government; some *attentiste* conservatives like

---

more than 600 to 5,340) just before the Tet offensive. Anyone familiar with revolutionary warfare should know, that even the most virtuoso revolutionary organization could not have pulled off the Tet offensive without massive, consistent, and covert support of the population in rural as well as urban areas. See Robert W. Komer, "Clear, Hold, and Rebuild," *Army* (May 1970), pp. 14-23, and "Pacification: A Look Back and Ahead," *Army* (June 1970), pp. 20-29.

[25] United States Senate Committee on Judiciary, Subcommittee to Investigate Problems Connected with Refugees and Escapees. *Refugee and Civilian War Casualty Problems in Indo-China: A Staff Report*, 91st Congress, 2nd Session. Sept. 28, 1970, pp. 4-5.

Deputy Ngo Cong Duc openly favor a provisional, coalition government of reconciliation which was proposed in Paris by the PRG as a move toward peace.

According to *The New York Times* (July 27, 1970), ARVN's rate of desertion was "up nearly 50 percent during the summer months of 1970" despite what officials termed the "morale building effects of recent operations in Cambodia." In Cambodia itself two paratrooper battalions of the expeditionary force "were operating with only 65 per cent of their man-power—the rest having deserted." General Do Cao Tri, Commander of the III Corps area which includes Saigon and leader of the Cambodian expedition, is reported to have been less conservative with his estimates. He told newsmen in Dalat that 75 per cent of his soldiers desert; of the remaining 25 per cent only 10 per cent wish to fight, and for every ARVN soldier killed in battle, nine desert.[26]

Meanwhile, *The New York Times* (October 19, 1970) disclosed a top-secret CIA report revealing that in response to Vietnamization the NLF had infiltrated some 30,000 cadres, reaching the highest levels of the Saigon government (including its secret services); that the "VC infrastructure" remained impenetrable; and that both conditions are predicated upon the complicity of the majority of the government's civilian and defense employees. The "disclosure" may have been meant to prepare the public for more repression and purges by the Saigon regime. But its significance is clear: its foreign trustees know that the regime, isolated from the people, is also hollow and eroding from within.

Even Sir Robert is reported to have returned gloomy from his recent mission to "Macedonia," as he unblushingly calls Vietnam. ("Come with me to Macedonia" he invites his readers in the Preface to *No Exit From Vietnam*, fancying his relationship to Mr. Nixon as the modern equivalent of the expert-advisers to Roman emperors.) The Phoenix (*Phung Hoang*) program has an actual score of zero: not one ranking member of the NLF is known to have been killed or captured, although this notorious "counter-terror" program is believed to have terrorized, tortured, and killed several thousand "suspects." No important defector has been received by the *Chieu Hoi* (Open Arms) program. In effect, it is the only

[26] For an account of the Qui Nhon riot, see *The New York Times*, December 4, 1970. For Luce's statement, see *Transcript WGBH/KECT The Advocates*, December 8, 1970. For an important statement by Ngo Cong Duc, see *The New York Review of Books*, November 5, 1970. For the revolutionaries' evaluation of the urban situation, see Jacques Decornoy's interview with Prime Minister Pham Van Dong, *Le Monde*, English Weekly, December 9, 1970. For General Tri's statement, *Africasia*, No. 27, (November 23, 1970), p. 37.

decent refugee resettlement program in Vietnam, for refugees with official connections generally get registered as defectors to get favorable treatment. Even the French had done better than that in Vietnam, and more so in Algeria. Yet in both places they had the wisdom and decency to negotiate withdrawal.

Such being the realities of Vietnamization, the U.S. government, intent on winning, could only mechanize the war. GI's are being replaced by airplanes, electronic devices, helicopter-gunships, long-range artillery, a variety of anti-personnel weapons, massive defoliation, crop destruction, and depopulation.[27] The details of these daily crimes and the extent of the damage they do are not and may never be completely known, especially since the U.S. government remains the primary source of information on these matters. A reading of the highly censored hearings (1969-1970) of Senator Symington's Foreign Relations Subcommittee on United States Security Agreements and Commitments Abroad gives a picture of the devastation caused by bombings in Indochina which are being carried out from American sanctuaries in Thailand, Okinawa, the Pacific Fleet, Guam, and Vietnam itself. By early 1970 there were some 3.5 million B-52 bomb craters scarring the landscape of Vietnam alone, the breeders and repositories now of germs and diseases. Occasionally, bombing statistics released by authorities and "authoritative sources" give a glimpse of its magnitude. The "mission" of bombings is not only to interdict supplies but also to destroy "personnel" (i.e., people) as Mr. Laird admitted early in August, even in the case of Cambodia.[28] The bombing of Indochina has exceeded several times the total tonnage dropped in all of World War II. As *The New York Times* editorially commented "the headlines gradually faded, but the air-war did not;" nor did the chemical war, nor helicopter-hunting, nor the gruesome anti-personnel weapons which maim so indiscriminately and leave so many disabled to care for.

If the population is to the guerrillas what water is to fish, the ultimate weapon of degenerate but powerful incumbents is to drain the water. That is the course that Mr. Johnson embarked on; Mr. Nixon is continuing the technological-attritive approach more skillfully and perhaps

[27] For a recent estimate of the extent and effects of chemical warfare in Indochina, see *The New York Times*, March 15, 1970, and May 24, 1970; *The Los Angeles Times*, December 31, 1970. Several scientific papers prepared by such eminent scientists as Meselson, Pfeiffer, Orians, Neilands, Mayers, and Galston, and sponsored by the American Association for the Advancement of Science, so far constitute the most reliable indicators of the effects of herbicides and other chemicals being used in Indochina.

[28] See Herbert Mitgang, "The Air War in Asia and Its Cover-up in Washington," *The New York Times*, August 31, 1970.

more consciously than did his predecessor. The policy may not be genocidal in intent; its goal appears to be attrition. And depending on how technically the word genocide is interpreted, it may not be in effect if it succeeds, but it will at least yield to the U.S. the beaten and sunken remainder of a once proud and brave people—a sort of 20th century Indian reservation in the heart of Asia.

In counter-insurgency, then, democratic "pluralism" is experienced by the targetted population in its corrupt, morally inverted form. In the "field" the different styles blend. The guerrillas and the masses experience all four: they are swept and bombed conventional style; punished and tortured *style-para;* quartered and controlled pacification style; and finally, face the prospects of a "long-haul, low-cost" technological extermination. In the lexicon of counter-revolutionaries, these wars are limited only in their consequences for the intervening power. For the people and country under assault, they are total.

The attitudes and assumptions which are shared by all believers in counter-insurgency may be summarized as follows.

1. There is a negative view of revolutionary warfare as a threat. Roger Hilsman (a well-known liberal scholar, associate of President Kennedy, and past Director of Intelligence and Research at the State Department) recalls that President Kennedy "let us all know of his interest in the subject and started us thinking about it. From the beginning of his administration the President was convinced that the *techniques* of 'revolutionary warfare' constituted a special kind of threat. . . ."[29] In an address to the National War College Vice-President Humphrey spoke of this "bold, new form of aggression which could rank with the discovery of gunpowder" as constituting "the major challenge to our security."[30] If guerrilla warfare is viewed as the latest enemy weapon, Vietnam is its testing ground. "If guerrilla techniques succeed in Vietnam," wrote James Reston, "nobody in Washington dare assume that the same techniques will not be applied in all communist rimlands from Korea to Iran."[31] It is this view of revolutionary warfare as a menacing technique, a weapon lethal to the interests of the U.S., that led counter-revolutionary scholars like W. W. Rostow to portray the invasion of Vietnam as a war to end wars. He told a University of Leeds audience that:

[29] Roger Hilsman, *To Move a Nation* (New York: Dell Publishing Co., 1967), p. 415. Emphasis mine.

[30] *The New York Times,* Serialized Editorials on "Wars of National Liberation," June 30, July 2, July 3, 1970.

[31] "Washington: The Larger Implications of Vietnam," *The New York Times,* April 25, 1965.

> ... if we have the common will to hold together and get on with the job—the struggle in Vietnam might be the last great confrontation of the post-war era. . . . If the Cuban missile crisis was the Gettysburg of the cold war, Vietnam could be the Wilderness; for, indeed, the cold war has been a kind of global civil conflict. Vietnam could be made the closing of one chapter in modern history and the opening of another.[32]

Since American interest in revolutionary warfare began with a counter-revolutionary posture, it is natural for its politicians and establishment academicians to be attracted more to the myths and methods of those who have had to defend themselves against guerrillas than to an understanding of the causes and characteristics of such a war. Americans are, therefore, unable to avoid the psychological and political pitfalls of colonial powers and feudal regimes. A symptom of this negativism is that, while describing it as a "bold new form of aggression," scholarly, no less than government publications, including the course books at Fort Bragg, generally avoid the term "revolutionary war" (except occasionally in single quotes) in favor of old terms which do not express the vital distinction between revolutionary and other types of guerrilla conflict. For example, the term "jungle warfare" is geographically limited, while "revolutionary wars" can be fought from the Sahara desert to the streets of Paris. "Guerrilla war" denotes some common features of such a conflict but does not emphasize the peculiarities of its modern, revolutionary variety. For example, like revolutionary wars, partisan movements known to us from the Napoleonic wars and World War II, were armed struggles led by guerrillas against a vastly superior enemy in which the overtly neutral but covertly engaged civilians provided the demographic "sea" to the guerrilla "fish." Yet the differences between these two types of warfare are significant. The partisans operated in support of conventional forces in open conflicts and expected liberation by the allies; they operated mostly as local bands which lacked nationwide structure and centralized direction; their aims were politically and socially limited to liberation. A revolutionary guerrilla movement on the other hand, seeks not simply to inflict military losses on the enemy, but to destroy the legitimacy of its government and to establish its own legitimacy through the creation of "parallel hierarchies" and a participatory, popular movement. The Chinese, Cuban, Algerian, and the Indochinese conflicts are cases in

[32] W. W. Rostow, "The Great Transition: Tasks of the First and Second Post War Generations," February 23, 1967. Similar views have been expressed by Mr. Nixon on several occasions including his May 14, 1969, speech on Vietnam.

point. Tito's partisan movement acquired many characteristics of a revolutionary war, but perhaps the earliest western example is the Irish rebellion of 1916-1922.

The negative posture precludes a correct understanding of the processes which explain, in the Third World today, the unprecedented popularity of armed revolutions, and the capacity of some to expand and sustain their struggles against incredibly heavy odds. Their purpose being counter-revolutionary, the theorists and practitioners of counter-insurgency are unable to grasp or unwilling to acknowledge the illegitimacy of incumbents, the finality of broken political and social links, and the forging of new ones. Recognition of the revolutionary process, its causes, creative thrust, inherent justice, and the achievement of legitimacy by a revolutionary movement must cost the counter-insurgents their *raison d'être*. Understandably then, counter-insurgents concentrate on studying and imitating the "techniques" and "tactics" of organizing and conducting revolutionary warfare, and betray a defective comprehension of the essence, the inner logic of revolutions. I. F. Stone has accurately described a peculiarity of the literature on counter-insurgency:

> In reading the military literature on guerrilla warfare now so fashionable at the Pentagon, one feels that these writers are like men watching a dance from outside through heavy plate glass windows. They see the motions but they can't hear the music. They put the mechanical gestures down on paper with pedantic fidelity. But what rarely comes through to them are the injured racial feelings, the misery, the rankling slights, the hatred, the devotion, the inspiration and the desperation. So they do not really understand what leads men to abandon wife, children, home, career, friends; to take to the bush and live gun in hand like a hunted animal; to challenge overwhelming military odds rather than acquiesce any longer in humiliation, injustice or poverty. . . .[33]

2. Counter-insurgents share a conspiratorial theory which views revolutionary warfare as being primarily a technical problem, i.e., a problem of plotting and subversion on the one hand and of intelligence and suppression on the other. As the chief conspiratorial group, the "Communists" are alleged to be the most likely initiators and beneficiaries of such revolutions. "Technique" is a key word in counter-insurgency. "We have a long way to go," Defense Secretary McNamara told a Congressional committee in 1963, "in devising and implementing

[33] I. F. Stone, *In Time of Torment* (New York: Vintage, 1968), pp. 173-174.

effective counter-measures against the communist techniques. But this is a challenge we must meet if we are to defeat the communists in this kind of war. It is quite possible that in the decade of the 1960's the decisive struggle will take place in this area."[34]

Given the preoccupation with technique, conduct of counter-insurgency is viewed as largely an exercise in the strategy and tactics of pacification and warfare, i.e., in managerial and military experimentations which come to be viewed as two facets of "one war." The military advantages of guerrillas—mobility, freedom from logistical anchors, good intelligence, surprise, etc.—are studied, and counter-measures and devices are developed. Irregular terrain is considered a primary condition for guerrilla warfare, as is the complicity of a coerced population. Therefore, counter-insurgent troops are trained in jungle warfare, and are taught and motivated to WHAM (Win Hearts and Minds).

This preoccupation has provided U.S. officials their only credible (in terms of facts), though less frequently expressed, justification for the invasion of Vietnam. In 1963, General Maxwell Taylor explained to a Congressional committee:

> Here we have a going laboratory where we see subversive insurgency, the Ho Chi Minh doctrine, being applied in all its forms. This has been a challenge not just for the armed services, but for several of the agencies of Government, as many of them are involved in one way or another in South Vietnam. On the military side, however, we have recognized the importance of the area as a laboratory. We have had teams out there looking at the equipment requirements of this kind of guerrilla warfare. We have rotated senior officers through there, spending several weeks just to talk to people and get the feel of the operation, so even though not regularly assigned to Vietnam, they are carrying their experience back to their own organizations.[35]

It is amazing that in a democracy, there was no serious public or parliamentary questioning of the consequences of an army considering another country a laboratory, and making a collective, psychic investment in it by rotating its senior officers. It is even more amazing that six years and at least four million casualties later, General Westmoreland could publicly declare in a civilized country that Vietnam had in fact been a valuable

[34] U.S. House of Representatives, Committee on Appropriations, Department of Defense Appropriations for 1963. Hearings, 87th Congress, 2nd Session, Part 2, pp. 49-50.

[35] Quoted in Committee of Concerned Asian Scholars, *The Indochina Story* (New York: Bantam Books, 1970), p. 93.

laboratory for testing new weapons and techniques; that the "lessons" and "devices" coming out of there are "revolutionizing" the techniques of warfare; that having inflicted in Vietnam "over two-thirds of enemy casualties," long-range artillery and air power had proved their capacity to "rain destruction anywhere on the battlefield within minutes..., whether friendly troops are present or not;" that with new electronic devices the enemy could be mechanically located, tracked, and targetted; and that technology would permit a "tremendous economy of man-power." The General is technically accurate; he may even be right in believing that "no more than ten years" separate us from the "automated battlefield."[36] If that is a correct prediction, American troop withdrawal may meet Sir Robert's timetable.

The trouble with the tracking, targetting, and locating devices, however, is that they are even less capable of distinguishing between civilians and combatants than are the GIs, for they cannot even distinguish between humans and animals. Such, for example, is the defect with the most favorite recent devices of counter-insurgency—the people sniffers. A *New York Times* article (May 28, 1967) notes: "that degree of exactitude would be welcome, but that is not the way the war is fought today. War Zone C and large areas of South Vietnam have been designated as free bombing zones. Anything that moves there is regarded as fair game. Previous high readings on the 'people sniffers' have brought B-52 raids from Guam." Some pacification purists disapprove of such weapons and their use. By so doing they only absolve themselves of responsibility in crimes of war, for the technological-attritive approach is the logical outgrowth of the interaction between counter-insurgency and technology. When a technologically superior country becomes committed to developing techniques against a people's war, it must end up producing and using weapons of mass murder. Given the frustrations of a protracted war, given also the imperative of avoiding American casualties, and the unwillingness of conscripted soldiers to fight for an unpopular regime, the distance between the Marine CAPS (Combined Action Platoons) and people sniffers was bound to be bridged by B-52s and free-fire zones.

The conspiratorial theory provides the needed rationale and justification for counter-insurgency and foreign interventions. The French theorists were notorious for ascribing all "insurgencies" to Communism. In their view Algeria's F.L.N. was a puppet alternately of Moscow, Peking,

[36] Congressional Record, October 16, 1969. *The New York Times*, October 15, 1969. Westmoreland's address was given at the Annual Meeting of the Association of the United States Army.

and Cairo, just as their American colleagues view the NLF as a puppet of North Vietnam and/or China. Even Sir Robert Thompson, the shrewdest and by popular acclaim the most cogent exponent of counter-insurgency, begins his first book with a discussion of Communism which, according to him, "was no real threat to *the security of the colonial governments or the well-being of the peoples of Southeast Asia*" until after World War II.[37] It is worth noting that in pairing the security of a foreign presence with the welfare of the natives, Sir Robert is not unique; his French and American counterparts share this propensity. Nor is the habit of viewing anti-colonial and radical nationalist movements as facets, or at least the dupes, of the international communist conspiracy uncommon, even among certified "anti-colonialist" American liberals.[38] The association of guerrilla warfare and radical nationalism with Communism helps justify U.S involvement in a wide range of counter-revolutionary operations from Ethiopia to Uruguay (the former against non-Marxist Eritrean nationalists, the latter against the Tupamaros, a group of anti-Communist Party, unorthodox radicals).

The insistence upon viewing revolutions in conspiratorial terms also permits a grossly distorted interpretation of the revolutionary process. For example, Sir Robert Thompson believes that the start and timing of an insurgency depends on an "order from Moscow." He notes that in liberated areas insurgents are "careful to reduce taxes on land and crops well below the government level or even to remit them for a period." "This," he explains, "they can afford to do, having no overhead, and still not lack for money."[39] The absence of overheads is not explained; and his suggestion that the Malayan Races Liberation Army and the NLF (Vietnam) are financially better off than their British and American opponents would be hilarious if it were not so cruel.

[37] Sir Robert Thompson, *Defeating Communist Insurgency* (London: Chatto and Windus, 1966), p. 14. (Italics added)

[38] E. L. Katzenbach, Deputy Under-Secretary of Defense in the Kennedy government wrote: "We have fought wars of urban and industrial interdiction, while our own Asiatic opponents *and the African opponents of our allies have patiently pursued a process of rural consolidation which has, in effect, given them an inviolable sanctuary from which they can attack and withdraw at will.*" Roger Hilsman presents a more sophisticated version: If armed revolutions result from international conspiracy, its nationalist expression must also have communist connections. The communists, says Mr. Hilsman, "*try especially hard to capture the extreme nationalists like Lumumba. They sponsor radical nationalism wherever they can find it.*" The message is clear: When a nationalist movement acquires radical content it is to be regarded as a threat to the "free world." (Italics added) See Lt. Col. T. N. Greene, editor, *The Guerrilla and How to Fight Him*, selections from *The Marine Corps Gazette*, (New York: Praeger, 1962), p. 21, 24.

[39] *Op. cit.*, p. 24.

3. A logical extension of the conspiratorial theory is the belief, held with particular tenacity by counter-revolutionary army officers, that any revolutionary movement is inspired, directed, and controlled from abroad. The sanctuary—from which guerrillas can smuggle supplies and in which they can train their troops—is considered the primary factor in their success. In a widely acclaimed speech in 1961, W. W. Rostow, Special Assistant to President Kennedy, stated that "we are determined to help destroy this international disease, that is, guerrilla war designed, initiated, supplied, and led from outside an independent nation."[40] Indeed so strong was the belief in the external origins of guerrillas that Washington promoted plans for the "offensive use of guerrillas" against undesirable regimes. Their performance in the Bay of Pigs and inside North Vietnam does not appear to have discouraged the enthusiasts.[41]

The importance of an active sanctuary should not be underestimated, particularly in cases when a great power intervenes with its full might. However, it is not essential to success. In Cuba, Yugoslavia, and China the revolutionaries did not have active sanctuaries. In Burma, and to a lesser extent in Greece, sanctuaries proved of limited value. Neither the extremely effective Morice Line in Algeria, nor the Lattre Line around the Red River Delta, nor the armored Ping-Han Japanese railroad in North China had much effect on the outcome of each war. Politically and militarily, revolutionary guerrillas are a self-sustaining group who make a fetish of self-reliance and can go on fighting indefinitely even if infiltration from across the border stops. There is overwhelming evidence that prior to massive U. S. escalation of the war, which necessitated the

[40] His statement appeared to threaten a land invasion, and foreshadowed the aerial invasion of North Vietnam: "It is important that the world become clear in mind that the operation run from Hanoi against Vietnam is as certain a form of aggression as the violation of the 38th parallel by the North Korean Army in June, 1950." Greene, *ibid.*, p. 59.

[41] Put into practice, these plans have ended disastrously. Such was the case with U.S. attempts to infiltrate guerrilla teams into North Vietnam, a practice that is believed to have begun in 1958 and continued at least until 1965. Bernard Fall, among others, has reported that these "[guerrillas] met with dismal failure. . . . Present losses are reported to run at 85 percent [of] the total personnel engaged in such operations." *The Two Viet-Nams* (New York: Praeger, 1964), second revised edition, p. 402. *The London Times* (April 20, 1968) reported that (a) the South Vietnamese agents were trained by the CIA in Special Forces camps, notably the 77th Special Forces group; (b) 95 per cent casualties were admitted in 1963 ("a complete fiasco"); and (c) these operations became a conduit for opium trade. Marshal Ky, who was in charge of the parachute drops, was removed for his part in opium smuggling.

For additional information on the "offensive use of guerrillas" see Slavko N. Bjelajac, "Unconventional Warfare in the Nuclear Era," *Orbis,* Vol. IV (Fall, 1960), pp. 323-337; Robert Strausz-Hupé, William R. Kitner, and Stefan T. Possony, *A Forward Strategy for America* (New York: Harper, 1961); and Peter Paret and John W. Shy, *Guerrillas in the 1960's* (New York: Praeger, 1962), pp. 4, 63-69.

augmentation of Northern aid, the NLF was entirely self-sufficient in South Vietnam; and that the bulk of its arms were captured or bought from Saigon. John Mecklin, a former U. S. senior diplomat in Saigon, put it quite succinctly when he stated that the interdiction of Northern supplies to South Vietnam would weaken the Vietcong "probably not much more than the efficiency of the Pentagon would be reduced if the air-conditioning were shut off."[42]

The incumbent or occupying army's pressure for conventional attack on an external sanctuary, however, is a good indicator that the war has been lost on home grounds. In revolutionary warfare professional armies trained for conventional combat follow a vicious logic of escalation which derives from acute frustration over an elusive war that puts in question not only their effectiveness, but the very validity of their training and organization. Moreover, the morale of professional soldiers cannot be maintained if they know they are fighting a popular revolution; hence, the compulsion to believe that behind the popular behavior lies the terror of an army trained, equipped, and directed by a foreign power, and the wish to draw the enemy into open battles. (Military officers often attest that they subject civilians to artillery fire and air raids in the hope that, deprived of civilian cover, the guerrillas would be forced into open battles.) Since reprisals against the population fail to produce the desired result, carrying the war to a sovereign nation becomes the most compelling and indeed, the only road to a conventional showdown with the enemy. In Algeria this demand led to French participation in the invasion of Suez, then to a single bombing raid of the Tunisian border town of Sakiet Sidi Youssef, which produced considerable international protest, including that of John F. Kennedy. Had the French government succumbed to the pressures of its army, France would have been the first power to violate the international practice of respecting the rights of sanctuary—a principle that was observed in Korea, Greece, Cyprus, and Malaya. We know what the U. S. might do if the Vietnamese were to bomb its sanctuaries in Thailand or the Pacific Ocean. But I wonder what position it will take as a major power when Portugal, Rhodesia, and South Africa follow its example and invade the African "sanctuaries" of their opponents. When practiced by a super-power, counter-insurgency involves the progressive breaking of the few rules which help keep potentially conflagrating conflicts within national boundaries.

4. The revolutionary movement is believed to enjoy considerable ad-

[42] John Mecklin, *Mission in Torment* (New York: Doubleday, 1965), p. 303.

vantage because in the words of W. W. Rostow "its task is merely to destroy while the government must build and protect what it is building."[43] Whether seriously held or consciously contrived, this view contradicts the findings of those who have studied and observed these movements. Given the inevitable, and generally vast, disparity of military strength between the guerrillas and the government, the success of a revolutionary movement depends on the covert and sustained support of a substantial portion of the population.

A revolutionary movement capable of eliciting such support must bring an ideological thrust, organizational form, and programmatic content into the amorphous revolutionary situation. It must demonstrate, in practice, that there are alternative structures and arrangements which approximate the popular yearning for a just, communal, and participatory system. A revolutionary guerrilla movement whose organization, leaders, and policies do not reflect the promises of the revolution (particularly in the base areas) is not likely to receive the sustained mass support necessary for protracted struggle. Achieving moral isolation of the enemy and legitimacy for the revolution requires not only the severance of the old but also the forging of new political and social links.

Once a revolutionary movement enters the guerrilla phase, its central objective is not simply to achieve the moral isolation of the enemy, but also to confirm, perpetuate, and institutionalize it by providing an alternative to the discredited regime through the creation of "parallel hierarchies." The major task of the movement, then, is not to outfight but to out-legitimize and outadminister the government. It must institute a measure of land reforms, reduce rents, equalize wages, and build an administrative structure to collect taxes, provide some education and social welfare, and maintain a modicum of economic activity. A revolutionary guerrilla movement which does not have these constructive concerns and structures to fulfill its obligations to the populace would degenerate into banditry. Even in clandestineness, the parallel government must prove its efficacy, and maintain a measure of accountability to the population. These are not easy tasks. It would be a rare revolutionary war, indeed, in which the government's destruction of civilian population and property does not surpass, by a wide margin, the losses caused by the guerrillas' selective terror and sabotage.

5. The liberal-reformist theorists of pacification bring to the doctrine of counter-insurgency a certain comprehension of the interdependence

[43] Greene, *op. cit.*, p. 60.

of political, military, and psychological factors in revolutionary warfare. They postulate that although guerrilla wars result from conspiracy and are waged by remote control, the cooperation or at least the neutrality of a passive population is essential to their survival and effectiveness. They recognize that politics play the dominant role in such conflicts and that for revolutionaries, civilians are the first and remain the primary object of attention. They admit the central importance of "ideology" and the existence of a "cause" around which the masses could be mobilized, and allow that the presence of acute economic and social grievances is causally linked with popular support for revolutionaries.

These theorists draw heavily on what they construe to be the revolutionary model. They search for a cause to match the enemy's. A counter-ideology is sought to compete with the revolutionary one. Strategic hamlets are the intended equals of popular base areas. Psychological warfare counters revolutionary political work. Pacification teams duplicate the revolutionary cadres. Re-education centers seek to reverse the guerrillas' commitment. The doctrine suffers from serious flaws, however. These result from its colonial antecedents, bureaucratic bias, and operational preoccupations. Their limited insight into the revolutionary process is dissipated by their obsession with mechanisms of control and by their continued focus on coercion as a means of obtaining popular support.

Since classical liberalism provides little justification for counter-revolutionary involvements abroad, pacification theorists seek it in related western traditions. This invariably entails a revival of the colonial and conservative ethos of the nation. They derive inspiration from colonial history and learn from its example. The French theorists, much like their American colleagues, emphasize that "pacification" is part of the western tradition, that conventional warfare gained ascendancy only during the two world wars, and that it was again being superceded by "limited," unconventional conflicts. In their search for western models and cultural continuity, the French theorists of *La Guerre Révolutionnaire* invoked the memories of pacification in the heyday of colonialism. They frequently cited examples and works of the colonizers of North Africa—General Bugeaud, Marshal Lyautey, and Galieni..The latter's doctrine on the identity of civilian and military authority, the role of *officier-administrateur* and *officier-éducateur* was extolled; their methods were emulated.[44]

In the U.S. the experiences with the Indians and other colonial exploits

[44] See Peter Paret, *French Revolutionary Warfare, From Indo-China to Algeria* (New York: Praeger, 1964), Chapter 7.

provide the source of inspiration. "It is ironic that we Americans have to learn this military lesson again in the twentieth century . . . ," wrote Roger Hilsman. After reminding his audience of American experiences in irregular warfare, in "Indian fighting," he invokes the memory of "one of the most successful counter-guerrilla campaigns in history" during the U.S. colonization of the Philippines. Mr. Hilsman goes on to give some gory details, and to draw some "fundamental lessons" from defeating the "extremists" and "bands of religious fanatics" who were vile enough to resist foreign occupation. The lessons include: (a) Maximum use of native mercenaries as demonstrated by the "fabulous exploits" of the "famed Philippine constabulary." (b) Leadership role for Americans—"over each group [of native recruits] we put a trained American officer—a bold and determined leader." (The official euphemism is "advisory role.") (c) Adoption of "Indian fighting" tactics of surprise and nighttime attacks—"the solution is to adopt the same weapons to fight him."[45] Mr. Hilsman does not mention that the "successful" Philippine campaign was ". . . the bloodiest colonial war (in proportion to population) ever fought by a white power in Asia; it cost the lives of 300,000 Filipinos."[46]

Despite their rhetoric, which stresses the primacy of politics and calls peaceful revolution their goal, the liberal-reformists treat counter-insurgency essentially as an administrative problem subject to managerial and technical solutions. A vulgar symptom of this phenomenon is that among the less sophisticated, second-rate counter-insurgency experts, managerial "innovations" become a fetish. Even changes in the size and appellation of platoons and pacification teams are viewed as innovations and improvements. Periodic changes in the abbreviations of essentially unchanged, artificial bureaucratic creations (RD, RF, PSDF, APT, APC and so on) give the "pacifiers" a sense of motion, which they equate with progress.[47] Ambassador Bunker has announced that CORDS (previously OCO and USOM) is now to be called CD and LDP (Community Defense and Local Development Plan).[48]

Even Sir Robert Thompson who evinces a keen understanding of some aspects of revolutionary warfare has a fundamentally bureaucratic view of the problem. "The bias of this book," he says in the introduction of his highly acclaimed first work, "is heavily weighted on the administrative and other aspects of an insurgency."[49] The promise is kept. He offers

[45] "International War: The New Communist Tactics" in Greene, *op. cit.*, p. 26.
[46] Fall, *op. cit.*, p. 464.
[47] For an example, see Robert Komer, *op. cit.*
[48] *The New York Times*, January 23, 1971.
[49] *Defeating Communist Insurgency*, *op. cit.*, p. 10.

a detailed and technically impeccable critique of the weaknesses and failings of counter-insurgency in Vietnam—cabinet-style government is lacking, the country is divided into too many provinces, hamlets are too small to be viable administrative units, the army has become larger than the police, security forces are fragmented, and strategic hamlets are not carefully planned and executed. Sir Robert's criticism is correct; but it is irrelevant, for no amount of bureaucratic wisdom could win the war in Vietnam. The relevant analysis would be concerned with the actual or potential legitimacy of the local as well as national authority represented by the Saigon regime, and with an honest appraisal of the causes and character of the linkages between the revolutionary movement and the Vietnamese masses. But the posture of counter-insurgency as well as the colonial and bureaucratic mentality preclude objectivity as well as the full perception of reality on these questions.

As noted earlier, revolutionary warfare demands the development of new styles and institutions before the attainment of power. In order to elicit voluntary and maximum participation by the people under conditions of extreme stress, the revolutionary leaders and cadres must form organic ties with them. Revolutionary style and institutions are most successful when they are qualitatively different from the existing ones, and, at the same time, appeal to the deepest and most natural yearnings of the masses. Revolutionary behavior, therefore, defies conventional styles and expectations. In revolutions, life begins to manifest itself in forms which are incomprehensible to bureaucrats and social engineers. Wolin and Schaar's analysis of the "educational bureaucracy" applies admirably to the counter-insurgency experts: "The bureaucratic search for 'understanding' does not begin in wonder, but in the reduction of the world to the ordinary and manageable. In order to deal with the world in the cognitive mode, the world must first be approached as an exercise in 'problem-solving.' " Finding the solution implies devising the right techniques; hence "reality is parsed into an ensemble of discreet though related parts, and each part is assigned to the expert specially assigned to deal with that part."[50]

Examples of the "reduction of the world to the ordinary and manageable" abound in the literature of counter-revolution. Only one should suffice: Professor Ithiel de Sola Pool rules out as "not acceptable . . . the inclusion of the Vietcong in a coalition government or even the persistence of the Vietcong as a legal organization in South Vietnam." This

[50] Sheldon Wolin and John Schaar, "Berkeley: The Battle of People's Park," *The New York Review of Books,* (June 19, 1969), p. 29.

yields him a problem: "the Vietcong is too strong to be simply beaten or suppressed." Whereupon cognitive dissonance theory suggests the solution: "discontented leadership" has "the potential for making a total break when the going gets too rough." The latter having been achieved by American fire power, the Vietcong need "a political rationalization for changing sides." Pacification must address itself to this task. The Vietcong's "image of reality" and "naive ideology" which regard the Saigon government as consisting of America's puppets and the peasants' exploiters must be replaced by a more realistic view. Toward this end reforms should be introduced, and the deserting Vietcong cadres should be given the opportunity to serve the government.[51] Professor Pool assumes that being bureaucrats on the "make" they will accept the opportunity to join the government. Dr. Pool is not a novice in political analysis; he is Chairman of the Political Science Department at M.I.T. Nor is he a stranger to Vietnam; over the years he has been conducting research there for the Pentagon. Yet, this is how he understands the dedication and motivation of the men who have successfully resisted, for more than two bloody decades, the fully employed might of one great power and one superpower. In counter-revolution, political analysis surrenders to the pathology of bureaucratic perception.

Students of French counter-insurgency have noted that the vast bibliography of *La Guerre Révolutionnaire* theorists contained no work on the ideology of the Algerian F.L.N. This observation is equally true of Vietnam, although Douglas Pike has seemingly devoted his attention to the organization and ideology of the NLF.[52] In fact, so pervasive has been the counter-revolutionary ethos of contemporary social science in the U.S. that the lack of attention to revolutionary ideology is generally true of contemporary liberal scholarship, i. e., if one understands ideology as the value commitment of a people, rather than as an administrative weapon. Richard Pfeffer has pointed out in connection with China studies:

> . . . the tendency to comprehend revolutions largely in terms of techniques of manipulation and control; and its corollary, the tendency to ignore, devalue, or treat primarily as a component of administration the force of revolutionary spirit, class struggle, and commitment. Missing in liberal scholarship's examination of revolution (and counter-revolution) has been the appreciation of the intense value commit-

[51] Quoted in Noam Chomsky, *American Power and the New Mandarins* (New York: Pantheon, 1967), p. 49.
[52] See Douglas Pike, *Vietcong* (Cambridge, Mass.: M.I.T. Press, 1966).

ment to radical change in a particular direction—just any direction will not do—held by those in revolt.[53]

Similarly, while the counter-revolutionaries display deep interest in revolutionary programs and organization, they perceive these as being motivated opportunistically and instrumentally. For example, land reform by revolutionaries is viewed as an opportunistic instrument for establishing control in the countryside, not as the positive outcome of the complex interaction between the revolutionary movement and the masses, nor the result of strongly held convictions, or deeply felt needs. The U.S. government's most renowned expert on Vietnam, writes of the NLF land reform: "In many cases this amounted to a virtual bribe; the rural Vietnamese was offered the thing he wanted above all else: Land."[54] He does not inform us why the GVN-U.S. has been unwilling or unable to offer a similar "bribe," nor what happens to the peasant's land when government control is re-established in a village. He also does not tell us why the U. S., with its enormous resources has failed in competing with the VC to buy-off the peasants.

It is only natural that their own opportunism, and preoccupation with stability and control should lead these theorists to at first *qualify*, then *distort*, and finally *abandon* their central, albeit only, positive theme—that revolutionary warfare has its basis in the existence of acute grievances, and that the achievement of social, economic, and political progress will reduce the chances of its outbreak and/or success. The qualification begins with the argument that although "modernization" is essential in the "long-run," social and economic inequities and injustices pose no real threat to stability until they are exploited by conspirators. The essential requirements of stability are, therefore, efficient administration and the policing of the population. Hence, reforms are seen only as useful auxilliaries to "pacification." Roger Hilsman concludes: "To summarize my feeling on popularity [of government], reform, and modernization: (1) they are important ingredients but are not the determinants of events; (2) their role must be measured more in terms of their contribution to physical security than we generally realize."[55] As the dialectic of pacification approaches its denouement, these qualifications provide the bases for the

[53] Richard M. Pfeffer, "Revolution and Rule: Where Do We Go From Here," *Bulletin of Concerned Asian Scholars*, (April-July 1970), Vol. 2, No. 3, p. 89, reviewing Ezra Vogel's *Canton Under Communism* (Cambridge, Mass.: Harvard University Press, 1969).

[54] Pike, *op. cit.*, p. 276.

[55] In Greene, *op. cit.*, pp. 31, 32.

emergence of a counter-revolutionary "revisionism"—totalitarian in precept, genocidal in effect. It postulates that the population's behavior, not its attitude, the revolutionary infrastructure's destruction, not the establishment of a government's popularity, are the operative factors in defeating "insurgency."[56]

The distortion develops, among other reasons, from continued focus on "coercion" and "terror" as the basis of mass support for guerrillas. At their best, counter-insurgency experts display an obvious contradiction between their rhetoric and their perception of reality. Sir Robert informs us that the "Communists are normally careful, however, not to murder a popular person before he has been discredited . . . are careful not to undertake general terror against the population as a whole. . . . Terror is more effective when selective. This allows the Communist behavior toward the people as a whole to be good and strict discipline is used to enforce it." Yet he describes this behavior as a "policy of wholesale murder . . . designed to keep the local population completely cowed."[57]

At their worst, some experts, among whom military men predominate, ascribe all the advantages of guerrillas to a "reign of terror." But the most pathetic are those who appear incapable of relating their facts to their interpretation. For example, Mr. Pike presents an impressive amount of evidence which illustrates that, except in the rarest instances, the NLF's use of sabotage and assassination is sociologically selective, politically judicious, and psychologically liberating. Yet his conclusions stand out in glaring opposition to his facts. One is struck by the schizophrenic quality of his study.

It is probably impossible for counter-revolutionaries to perceive the truth, for doing so entails admitting a revolution's legitimacy, and their own side's lack of it. Even Sir Robert's statement contains more than mere rhetorical exaggeration. He views effective coercion of the people as the main purpose of "selective terror." These attitudes provide the justification for a government's "counter-terror" which begins with "selective" reprisals only to escalate into massive and indiscriminate violence.

The complex reality behind "terror" is contrary to these views. By reason of its clandestineness and dependence on the masses for secrecy and information, the guerrilla movement cannot compete with the coercive ability of the legal government, or the occupying power. Highly committed but covert civilian support cannot be obtained at gun-point.

[56] The term "revisionist" in this context is credited to David Halberstam, although he used it to apply only to the question of land reform. See his "Voices of the Vietcong," *Harper's*, (January 1968), p. 47.

[57] *Defeating Communist Insurgency*, *op. cit.*, pp. 24, 25.

Given their low estimate of the masses, incumbents belatedly discover that their "counter-terror" produces results quite opposite of those expected or desired. This realization increases their frustration and feeling of moral isolation. Instead of providing a basis for correction, this belated and hazy perception of reality only augments their desperation and leads to incredible acts of inversion. Thus, the bombing and burning of villages are often justified on the ground that the affected villagers will blame the Vietcong for "exposing" them to government reprisals; it is believed that the enemy thus loses popular support.

Since they are interested only in operational payoffs, the counter-insurgents' investigation into revolutionary theory and practice tend to be selective, superficial, and systems-oriented. For example, the military writings of Mao Tse-tung are reproduced and cited out of their political context, their specific, local character is ignored, and Mao is presented as a system-builder, rather than the leader of a historical revolution.[58] The "systems" orientation as well as the conspiratorial view produce a bias in favor of seeking similarities among revolutions. Hence, the fact that, despite many similarities, the Chinese, Vietnamese, Algerians, and Cubans fought very different wars and owed little to Mao's "doctrine" is often ignored. Yet the same theorists rarely acknowledge the fact that the similarities among those revolutions result more from common conditions (e.g., Japanese, French, and American occupation) than a common doctrine or source of conspiracy.

The counter-revolutionary theorists are ultimately concerned with order more than participation, control more than consent of the governed, obedience more than title to authority, stability more than change. To them the people are objects of policy, a means rather than an end, a manipulable, malleable mass whose behavior toward the government is ultimately more important than are their feelings and attitudes. It is only natural that counter-revolutionary theorists should dissipate their limited insight into revolutionary warfare as they focus on the links between the people and the revolutionary cadres. They conclude that the effectiveness and strength of revolutionaries rest in their ability to manipulate ("techniques of mass deception") and coerce the masses ("terror"), and in their ruthless organizational skills ("infrastructure"). As a result, their prescriptions reveal considerable technical expertise, an obsession with controlling and manipulating the masses (strategic hamlets, Psy-Warfare), and an

[58] For example, see E. L. Katzenbach, Jr., "Time, Space, and Will: Politico-Military Views of Mao Tse-tung," Greene, *op. cit.*, pp. 11-21. The writer goes so far as to ascribe the battle of Dien Bien Phu directly to Mao's "daring." (p. 21)

oblique if not altogether distorted view of the needs and demands of the people. Their indebtedness to what they construe to be the insurgent model is unmistakable; but their understanding of it remains crooked. The "reflection in the mirror is sharp," wrote Peter Paret of the French counter-revolutionary doctrine in Algeria, "while the thing reflected remains shadowy."[59] And so we return to Stone's classic description of these men "... watching a dance from outside through heavy plate glass windows. They see the motions but they can't hear the music...."

In practice the liberal-reformists seek to wage counter-revolutionary campaigns by adopting the organizing principles, "attitudes," and "behavior" of the revolutionaries. Sir Robert calls it the "Same Element Theory of Guerrilla Warfare." He advises engaging guerrillas "in their own element" by inserting government forces "into the same element as the insurgent forces to which they are opposed." A fierce dog cannot beat a tom-cat in an alley, for the latter will "climb up the tree and leave the dog to chase female cats." The answer, says Sir Robert, is to use instead a fiercer tom-cat; "the two cannot fail to meet because they are both in exactly the same element and have exactly the same purpose in life. The weaker will be eliminated."[60]

Sir Robert presupposes the incumbent government's legitimacy, justice, and willingness to accomplish the transformation of society. Without such an assumption it would surely be impossible to assign to counter-insurgent forces "exactly the same purpose in life" as that of the revolutionaries; or to expect that the population-at-large will provide the demographic sea to the counter-guerrilla fish. Yet barring a negotiated or unilateral abdication and withdrawal (the latter in the case of a foreign power), incumbents are by definition incapable of seriously seeking the removal of the causes upon which a successful revolution may be based. France, the U.S.A., and their local collaborators could not credibly claim national liberation to be their goals in Algeria and Vietnam. Algerian *colons* and Vietnamese landlords who formed the backbone of incumbency could not be serious about instituting meaningful land reforms.

Lacking genuine revolutionary, even reformist, commitment, unable or unwilling to acknowledge the real aspirations of the people, the counter-revolutionary effort misses the heart of the matter. Hence, they progressively give up on winning the hearts; and concentrate instead on conquering the minds ("it's the minds that matter," says Sir Robert) and

[59] Paret, *op. cit.*, p. 20.
[60] *Defeating Communist Insurgency*, *op. cit.*, pp. 119-120.

destroying bodies. Even Sir Robert, now retired from a relatively civilized colonial civil service and only a part-time missionary to "Macedonia," has been unable in his most recent book to escape the vicious logic of protracted counter-insurgency. Others, being less civil and more service-minded, may be even less fortunate; for unlike Sir Robert, they do not feebly condemn or even acknowledge the GVN-U.S. practices of "torture and the shooting of prisoners" and of using weapons of "mass destruction . . . in inhabited areas."[61] It is a nemesis of the liberal-reformist approach that it breeds among its believers and practitioners a contempt for the very liberal values and democratic institutions which they claim to represent. A closer look at the paradigm of counter-revolutionary practice in Algeria and Vietnam would lead us to the conclusion that the failure to transform the "fierce dog" into a "tom-cat" produces a frustrated animal endowed with neo-fascist attributes and genocidal tendencies.

* * * *

In Vietnam, more than in Algeria, the doctrine of counter-insurgency has had its full play. In both countries its inner logic and corrupt and destructive nature was fully exposed to the world, stripped of the liberal, reformist pretenses of its practitioners. Yet there might be a fateful difference between Algeria and Vietnam. The former marked the end of France's involvement in counter-insurgency; its exponents ended up in prison or oblivion. The latter appears to have been a testing ground and training area rather than the terminal point for American counter-revolution. Its practitioners attend conferences and join public forums to discuss the "lessons" of Vietnam. There is little reason to hope that the U. S. will soon end its policy of military support and interventions in behalf of the status quo in Asia and Latin America. Its officials are known to count among the benefits of the Vietnam war the unusual opportunity to develop and test new weapons for "irregular" warfare; a new generation of officers and men have gained combat experience in guerrilla warfare in unfamiliar terrain; lessons learned in Vietnam have led to improved techniques of pacification in the client states of Asia and Latin America. Developments in Indonesia, Thailand, Guatemala and, above all, in Laos and Cambodia, are indications that the "lessons" of Vietnam have reinforced the most barbaric and destructive components of counter-insurgency. The technological-attritive approach is now likely to be practiced in its latest, revised form which stresses the establishment of totalitarian controls over the population, massive displacement and dispossession of the

[61] *No Exit From Vietnam, op. cit.*, p. 164.

peasants, and rapid and ruthless reprisals with maximum reliance on technology—bombings, napalm, and defoliation—rather than troops.

At a conference on Violence and Social Change, organized by the Adlai Stevenson Institute in the summer of 1969, Robert W. Komer, former Ambassador in charge of the American Pacification Program in Vietnam, explained that Vietnam had proved the inefficacy of "gradual escalation" which permitted the "guerrillas to make adjustments" and withstand allied pressure. Hence, the "lesson" was to escalate ruthlessly and rapidly; "snow them under," he said. It is a measure of the helplessness of humanity rather than of freedom in America that in my concern for the survival of the Indochinese people and culture I should have to share public platforms with men who, in the opinion of qualified persons, are at least deserving of trial as criminals of war.

Conclusion. There are many ways in which the practice of counter-insurgency erodes the democratic processes and institutions of metropolitan countries. The fall of the Fourth Republic, the French army officers' involvement in the clandestine OAS, and their open rebellion in 1962 are examples for Americans to ponder. The pursuit of counter-revolutionary foreign policy undermines a democracy in many ways. It enhances the power of the secret services of government over which parliamentary institutions can exercise little or no control and whose activities public organs (press, political parties, etc.) are normally unable to report and censure. The expanded role of the CIA, and of the armed forces' special branches are examples. As their activities and influence increase, such agencies not only circumvent representative institutions but even begin to infiltrate and corrupt civilian life. The CIA's clandestine use of the National Students Association and of several universities is a case in point.

In order to overcome the checks of parliamentary institutions and public opinion, a government involved in counter-insurgency seeks ways to reduce its accountability to representative bodies, and to by-pass pressures of public opinion. Expansion of the role of the secret services is only one of many ways in which this is done. Another favorite ploy is to employ puppet armies and experts to subvert foreign governments and fight wars by proxy. This is how Mr. E. L. Katzenbach stated the proposition in an anthology which received the approbation of President Kennedy:

> . . . we need not only troops which can strike on the peripheries of the free world, but also troops which can be sent not merely to fight but also to maintain order. *We need not only useful troops but usable troops—that is to say, troops which are politically expendable,* the

> kind of troops who can do the job as it is needed without too great a political outcry in a nation like our own which so abhors war. . . .[62]

The emphasis on "usable troops" led the French to rely heavily not only on special units of enlisted men (e.g., the parachutists) and on African regiments but also, and increasingly, on the mercenary Foreign Legion units which were largely composed of Germans. The U.S., in addition to providing armaments, training, and "advisers" to counter-revolutionary clients, raises private armies like that of the Cuban exiles who invaded Cuba or the Guatemalan rightists who have in recent years terrorized the peasants. In their Special Warfare units, they have also been recruiting Central and Eastern European exiles. A counter-revolutionary policy abroad can only reinforce reactionary trends within a society. It cuts a foreign power off from progressive forces and influences abroad, locks it in rigid alliances with reactionary elements, and encourages the rise and recruitment in the government of ultra-conservative and fascist elements.

Failure to defeat revolutionaries in protracted war alienates participants in counter-insurgency against the democratic values and institutions of their own country. The war is eventually seen as being lost at home rather than in the field; dissent and divisions at home contrast with the enviable solidarity and dedication of the enemy; and democratic institutions increasingly appear as unworkable in revolutionary settings. The "powerlessness" of the "democratic ideology" was the common complaint among the supporters of counter-insurgency in France. In America too it is becoming a familiar theme, in scholarly analyses no less than political pronouncements. One frequently sees statements similar to the following by Professor Ithiel de Sola Pool:

> The agonizing political lesson that racks this country is that there has been a failure of our own political system. The intensity of dissent, the lack of public understanding of our national policy, and the divisions that rack American society today have thrown into some question the stability of government in the United States, the capacity of our system to govern effectively, the basic commitment of the American people to the payment of costs of our national goals. These are failings of which we usually accuse the Vietnamese, but the criticism is more fairly addressed against ourselves[63]

[62] Greene, *op. cit.*, p. 21. (Italics added)
[63] Richard M. Pfeffer, *No More Vietnams?* (New York: Harper and Row, 1968), p. 142.

Disaffection from the existing system occurs also among the opponents of counter-revolutionary war since their protests produce no result, and new elections, while producing new promises, fail to yield a new policy. The divisions and disillusionments that follow involvement in counter-revolution ultimately reduce the legitimacy of existing institutions, inspire opposition to or contempt for them, and weaken the will to resist their corruption or destruction.

Above all, involvement in counter-insurgency politicizes the military and encourages its intrusion into civilian life. In France it produced, at first, deep extra-constitutional involvement by the military in the political affairs of the country, and finally a rebellion. Training and participation in counter-insurgency necessarily involves emphasis on the identity and interrelatedness of civilian and military tasks and authority. It is not realistic to expect military men who are trained to be "soldier-political workers" to remain apolitical at home. The maintenance of a double standard for the army's role abroad and at home becomes especially difficult when the war is seen as being lost at home. The determination to equip the natives with the "will to fight" transfers eventually to the metropolitan country when the "will" of the people "at home" appears to be sagging. The crusade abroad may find expressions at home when the society is viewed as needing moral or political regeneration.

The counter-revolutionary chickens, therefore, have a tendency to return home to roost. Whether the "homecoming" is complete or partial depends on the strains and stresses of involvements abroad, and a government's ability to extricate itself from the war in good time. The Fourth Republic survived the first Indochinese war but collapsed during the Algerian. It is impossible to tell how many more Vietnams the American republic can sustain. There is, however, considerable evidence that the forces of law and order, including the army and several local police departments are applying the theories of pacification and counter-guerrilla warfare to the problems at home. In recent years the Army and Marine Corps have been engaged in research (and presumably training) in "urban-guerilla warfare." In 1968 a Directorate of Civil Disturbances was established in the Department of the Army, and the Pentagon now houses a Situation Room for domestic disturbances.

Less easy to identify but more pervasive are the influences which the climate created by involvement in counter-insurgency has on the attitudes toward, and styles of dealing with, political problems at home. The treatment, in recent years, of dissenters in America is probably not unrelated to the war in Vietnam. Official violence against demonstrators in

Chicago during the Democratic Party convention is one example. Most recently, during the demonstrations for Peoples' Park in Berkeley, helicopters were used to spray the demonstrators with a variety of gas (CS) which is widely used in Vietnam but which is outlawed by the Geneva Conventions. The commander is reported to have regretted the "discomfort and inconvenience to innocent by-standers," adding that "It is an inescapable by-product of combating terrorists, anarchists, and hard core militants on the streets and on the campus."[64] Alameda County's Sheriff Madigan explained that "We have a bunch of young deputies back from Vietnam who tend to treat prisoners like Vietcong."[65] One can only hope that this does not constitute a preview of things to come.

[64] Wolin and Schaar, *op. cit.*, p. 25.

[65] From Robert Sheer's eyewitness account of Santa Rita Jail, *Ramparts*, (August 1969), pp. 50-51.

ROBERT W. KOMER

Impact of Pacification on Insurgency in South Vietnam

I. *Introduction*

Whatever one's views about U.S. policy toward Vietnam or U.S. performance in that tragic conflict, in at least one respect the U.S. consciously attempted not to overmilitarize or over-Americanize the war, but attempted rather to cope with its rural revolutionary and largely political dimension. This attempt has had many names; the most widely known (though hardly the most apt) is pacification.

From Diem's Agrovilles in 1959 through the Strategic Hamlet program of 1961-1963, Diem's Civil Guard, and the Revolutionary Development program of 1965-1966, many promising though regretably modest experi-

---

Ambassador Komer served as Deputy for Civil Operations and Revolutionary Development Support (CORDS) to the Commander, United States Military Assistance Command, Vietnam (COMUSMACV), and as chief pacification adviser to the Government of Vietnam in 1967 through 1968. He then went to Turkey as U.S. Ambassador. Before going to Vietnam, he was a senior member of the National Security Council staff from 1961 to 1965, Deputy Special Assistant to the President for National Security Affairs from 1965 to 1966, and the Special Assistant to President Johnson in charge of supervising the "other war" of pacification in Vietnam. He was awarded the Presidential Medal of Freedom in December, 1967, and the Secretary of State's Distinguished Honor Award in November, 1968. He is currently doing research at The RAND Corporation.

Prepared for delivery at the Sixty-sixth Annual Meeting of The American Political Science Association, Biltmore Hotel, Los Angeles, California, September 8-12, 1970.

ments were tried. But not until the so-called "new model" pacification program of 1967 was the effort made on a sufficiently large and comprehensive scale—and sustained consistently over a sufficient period—to provide any full-scale test of its potential in coping with rural insurgency. Moreover, it was the only program carried out when the tide was running in favor of, rather than against, the Government of Vietnam (GVN) (thanks to massive U.S. military intervention at horrendous cost), thus permitting a sustained expansion into enemy-held and contested rural areas. For these reasons, this article will focus on the 1967-1970 pacification effort.

Unfortunately, the open literature on Vietnam pacification efforts in general and the 1967-1970 effort in particular is exceedingly thin.[1] Despite the millions of words written about Vietnam since 1965, there is a notable dearth of systematic analysis of such key aspects as the pacification program. This aspect of the Vietnam tragedy has been consistently neglected in favor of the more dramatic aspects of the war. A survey of press and periodical reporting over the three years of 1966-1968 reveals very few articles annually that even attempt to deal with pacification in the round. Most open sources available to the academic community seem quite impressionistic, particularly on the 1967-1970 period when commentaries on pacification almost invariably became caught up in the growing controversy about the war. An adversary proceeding developed—indeed a vicious circle—wherein the more the establishment attempted to show that progress was occurring the more the media and other critics attempted to show that it was all a house of cards. Hence, this article will be based primarily upon the author's personal experience and access to operational data during the period. This necessarily entails a certain parochial bias. However, most of the data on the impact of the current program is of comparatively recent origin, since it only began to gather momentum with the first Accelerated Pacification Campaign of November 1968-January 1969, and the cumulative results have become fully apparent only in 1969-1970.

[1] The most coherent analysis of one phase of Vietnam pacification is by William A. Nighswonger, *Rural Pacification in Vietnam* (New York: Praeger, 1966). But it covers only the period before the major "new model" pacification program got underway. Most open literature is on pre-1966 pacification efforts. See for example the brief but perceptive accounts in George Tanham, editor, *War Without Guns: American Civilians in Rural Vietnam* (New York: Praeger, 1966). The most comprehensive account of the current program is the extensive testimony of Ambassador W. E. Colby and his CORDS colleagues before the Senate Foreign Relations Committee in February 1970 (which has not yet been published by the Committee). For a summary of 1966-1970, see R. W. Komer, "Clear, Hold, and Rebuild," *Army* (May 1970), pp. 16 24, and its companion piece, "Pacification: A Look Back and Ahead," *Army* (June 1970), pp. 20-29.

II. *Nature of the "New Model" Pacification Program, 1967-1970*

Since there is so little in the open literature, it seems worthwhile to summarize the 1967-1970 Vietnam pacification program as a prerequisite to assessing its impact. It differed in many significant respects from previous pacification efforts, in Vietnam or elsewhere.

Conceptually, all Vietnam pacification efforts have been designed essentially to serve two constructive aims: (1) sustained protection of the rural population from the insurgents, which also helps to deprive the insurgency of its rural popular base; and (2) generating rural support for the Saigon regime via programs meeting rural needs and cementing the rural areas politically and administratively to the center. A secondary purpose has been to help neutralize the active insurgent forces and apparatus in the countryside. In essence, then, it is a civil as well as military process.

The 1967-1970 program differs from its predecessors less in concept than in the comprehensive nature and massive scale of the effort undertaken, and in the *unified management* which pulled together a great variety of subprograms for the first time on a fully countrywide scale. It must also be seen as a product of the circumstances and constraints existing at the time. It came late in the day, and only after costly U.S. military intervention had averted final collapse of the coup-ridden GVN and had created a favorable military environment in which the largely political competition for control and support of the key rural population could begin again. This competition was also facilitated by the increased stability at the center afforded by the Ky-Thieu regime. But the previous deterioration of the chronically weak GVN administration and security apparatus in the countryside made pacification an uphill task from the start. The new program also entailed a painful build-up and deployment of resources, which took at least two years. All this necessitated a crash effort, as did the time constraints uppermost in U.S. policy-makers' minds. Few expected that the U.S. public would sit still for a slow, methodical ten-year campaign.

Since most available resources were in Vietnamese and U.S. military hands by 1967, since pacification required first and foremost the restoration of security in the countryside, and since what little GVN administration that existed outside Saigon had become military dominated, it was also logical for the new pacification program to be put under military auspices. On the U.S. side the result was a hybrid "Rube Goldberg" type of civil-military advisory organization called Civil Operations and Revolutionary Development Support (CORDS). Paradoxically, CORDS resulted in far greater civilian influence on the pacification process than would otherwise have been likely, since civilians occupied most top CORDS positions.

Even though the U.S. made a major advisory, logistic, and financial contribution, the "new model" pacification program has remained primarily Vietnamese from the outset. With one or two minor exceptions, all operational programs were staffed and managed by Vietnamese. The Vietnamese-to-U.S. adviser ratio at the peak of U.S. involvement was over 100 to 1. Of course, this was made possible (especially on the security side) because during 1966 to 1969 the U.S. military assumed the chief offensive role against the Viet Cong/North Vietnamese Army, (VC/NVA)—except in IV Corps—thus permitting the allocation of South Vietnamese military resources to providing local security in the countryside. On the other hand, the very fact that pacification was essentially a Vietnamese enterprise entailed another series of constraints:

> Some have criticized the pacifiers for adopting over-simplified massive quantitative approaches to a highly sensitive task. In my view, this was the only feasible way to get early countrywide impact, given the extent of the need, the limited quality of the resources available, the GVN's limited administrative capabilities and the lateness of the day. It is worth remembering that effective countrywide pacification had eventually to encompass [over] 10,000 hamlets [and] 2,000 villages [in] 250 districts and 44 provinces. The GVN could not afford politically to neglect half the country, or ignore certain provinces, in order to concentrate on the rest. Moreover, some resources existed in all these provinces that might as well be utilized since they were not readily transferable. Providing sustained rural security on this vast scale was inevitably a manpower extensive matter, almost requiring simple mass approaches. We were vividly aware of a major weakness in previous pacification efforts: the securing troops stayed only briefly and then moved on, after which the hamlets often retrogressed.
>
> It must also be borne in mind that pacification was a 99 percent Vietnamese program, and properly so, even though supported by the United States. We pacifiers, coming along late in the day, had to make do with some of the most poorly trained and equipped Vietnamese assets that no one else was really using. Moreover, we couldn't design programs beyond the capabilities of such Vietnamese administrative structure as was left by 1967, never strong but further degraded by terror and war. Lastly, it didn't take Tet 1968 and its aftermath to make us realize in the field that we didn't have five or ten years to get pacification moving. By 1967-68 the time seemed past for long-term programs or slow oilspot techniques.
>
> We further realized that there was no one pacification technique that could of itself and by itself be decisive if we just put all our resources

behind it. So as a practical matter we pulled together all the various programs then in operation–civilian and military–that looked as though they could make a contribution. To utilize all available resources we pushed multiple programs simultaneously, though according to a realistic set of priorities. In effect, we pragmatically sought to build the new model pacification on existing assets, as a concerted series of admittedly inefficient countrywide programs, which nonetheless seemed capable of gradual improvement to the point where they cumulatively offered hope of saturating the enemy and enabling us to build faster than he could destroy. Given the real-life circumstances of wartime Vietnam, the war's chaotic impact on a society still half-formed, and the elusive yet all-pervasive enemy presence, making quantity substitute for quality was almost the only realistic approach. Indeed, I recall no highly efficient program in Vietnam–no single American or Vietnamese effort that would be regarded as such by American standards.[2]

Providing Territorial Security. Pragmatically, the multifaceted 1967-1970 pacification program is perhaps best described in terms of its components. A notable feature was the stress on sustained territorial security (local clear and hold) as the indispensable first stage of pacification. Earlier pacification efforts had partly foundered on the lack of this. The military—regarding pacification as civilian agency business—had never provided adequate security resources. Nighswonger finds this a major source of the failure of earlier programs. From his own experience he saw the "heart" of pacification as "protection of the peasant," and he concluded in 1966 that "a rural security system is only an urgent need, but not yet a reality in Vietnam."[3] This was recognized in the imaginative Revolutionary Development (RD) program of 1966-1967. Its cutting edge, the 59-man, RD Cadre team, was designed as an armed paramilitary force to provide protection as well as developmental help to the hamlet. Also relevant was the allocation of 40 to 50 Army of the Republic of Vietnam (ARVN) battalions to provide temporary security in selected RD campaign areas in the 1967 pacification plan.

But large-scale pacification required full time *sustained protection* at the key village/hamlet level on a scale far beyond that which could be provided by these expedients. The pacification planners saw the long neglected Regional and Popular Forces (RF and PF) as the logical force-in-being on which to build. They were all locally recruited, and the bulk

[2] Komer, "Pacification," *ibid.*, p. 24.
[3] Nighswonger, *op. cit.*, pp. 70, 130, 147.

of them were volunteers (partly in order to avoid the draft). RF served only in their own provinces and PF in their own districts. The placing of the RF/PF advisory effort under the new U.S civil-military pacification management, CORDS, in conjunction with the Republic of Vietnam Armed Forces (RVNAF) reorganization of 1967 marked the beginning of a truly integrated civil-military pacification program on a major scale. At long last, primary responsibility for local protection of the rural population devolved upon local forces recruited from this population itself.

The RF/PF were re-equipped and upgraded, their command clearly placed under province and district chiefs, and their numbers greatly increased. They expanded by more than 100,000 in 1968 alone, and now number some 510,000 men in over 1500 RF companies and 6000 PF platoons. The Tet shock of 1968 led to revival of another local security mechanism, the part-time People's Self-Defense Forces (PSDF). These have grown to over three million, equipped with some 500,000 weapons. Though PSDF have often engaged the enemy, their most useful role is probably less in local defense than as a means of engaging the population politically in anti-VC activity.

Two other pacification sub-programs were designed to help cut into insurgent strength. A revitalized *Chieu Hoi* program aimed both at inducing VC to rally to the GVN and then at employing them productively. Ex-VC ralliers are now used in a wide variety of military as well as civil pacification roles. The GVN's *Phung Hoang* (Phoenix) program aimed at neutralizing the clandestine VC politico-administrative apparatus, which many regard as the key to their insurgent capabilities. The VC infrastructure (VCI) taxes, proselytizes, propagandizes, and terrorizes the rural population; recruits and controls VC local forces; and administers VC-controlled areas. To date *Phung Hoang* has been a small, poorly managed, and largely ineffective effort, though some attrition of the VCI has taken place.

Civil Programs. The other major aspect of the "new model" pacification effort has been the many civil programs aimed primarily at: (1) the revival of a modestly functioning rural administration; (2) rural economic revival to provide pragmatic incentives to the farmer; and (3) the establishment of other essential rural services, such as medical and educational facilities, refugee care, and a civil police presence. Many of these programs, inherited from the USAID mission, were integrated into a comprehensive pacification scheme by the GVN Central Pacification Council and CORDS.

Perhaps most significant has been the concerted GVN/U.S. effort *to restore village/hamlet self-government,* which was abolished by Diem in 1956. During the 1967-1970 period, a series of GVN decrees were promulgated, and pragmatic steps were taken to provide for the election of hamlet chiefs and village councils, the creation of autonomous village budgets, and the reservation of local taxing powers and use of local tax revenues to the village. Moreover, GVN decree #045 of 1 April 1969 placed local security forces and police under the village chief's authority for the first time in history, and lodged responsibility for framing local self-help plans in the village itself. Also in 1969, the GVN granted each elected village council a one million piaster village self-development fund under control of the village council itself.[4]

The RD Cadre program, which grew to a peak of 47,000 men in some 750, 59-man teams, and its associated New Life Development (later Village Development) program under the RD Ministry were used largely to strengthen local government and to assist in self-help projects. Another facet of the effort to restore functioning local government has been the continuing purge since late 1967 of corrupt or ineffective military district and province chiefs; the purge has touched most provinces and districts in South Vietnam.

A major parallel effort, given high priority from 1968 on, was the *revival of the rural economy,* which for years had suffered the chief brunt of the war. War-induced boom conditions and greater security were enhancing the urban sector of the economy while the rural sector was ever more depressed. A combination of techniques was introduced to close this urban-rural gap; among them, changing the terms of trade between urban and rural sectors by increasing prices paid to the crop producers, large-scale introduction of new IR-5 and IR-8 rice strains, accelerating import and distribution of fertilizer, expanding protein and free grain output, and not least, reopening and upgrading of key roads and waterways utilizing military engineers and U.S. contractors. Rural taxes were abolished, along with a web of economic and resource control restrictions. Water pumps and tractors were introduced in large numbers. In June 1970 a far-reaching land reform program finally passed the National Assembly, and the GVN is laying plans to redistribute 200,000 hectares of land per year for the next several years.

Other pacification programs also gathered momentum between 1967

[4] See *The Vietnamese Village 1970: A Handbook for U.S. Advisers,* Community Development Directorate, CORDS MACV, 2 May 1970.

and 1970. Greatly increased resources were devoted to refugee care and, more recently, *refugee resettlement*. The USAID-supported hamlet school and teacher-training program was continued and broadened. There was a major effort to improve rural hospital and dispensary facilities. The GVN's feeble propaganda capabilities were strengthened, but more important, the widespread use of radio (and even some television) in rural areas gave the GVN a virtual monopoly of mass communications. The effort to provide a civil law-and-order capability by strengthening the feeble National Police was also stepped up, and in 1969 police again were being stationed in the villages.

Two other distinctive features of the 1967-1970 pacification program were unified civil-military single management (for the first time), and a massive increase of resource inputs. Total pacification funding by the U.S. and GVN rose almost threefold from roughly $582 million in 1965 to over $1.5 billion scheduled in 1970 (dollar equivalents), including military outlays (the largest single is RF/PF funding). By 1970 roughly half of the real cost of pacification was borne by the GVN. Unified management of these outlays and of the multiplicity of pacification activities in several thousand villages and hamlets was feasible only by creating stronger central management at Saigon, region, province, and district levels.

Once again, the purpose here is not to represent the pacification effort of 1967-1970 as a highly efficient, high-impact program; it made no such pretense. Like most things in Vietnam, it has been cumbersome, wasteful, poorly executed, and only spottily effective in many respects. The aim is rather to describe the major differences between the "new model" and previous programs in management, size, and program emphasis. Nonetheless, GVN and U.S. efforts in 1967-1970 did manage to convert some innovative but small-scale experiments into a coherent, integrated, civil-military program on a big enough and consistent enough scale to produce gradually significant impact on Viet Cong prospects in the countryside. Whatever its faults, the 1967-1970 program at least stands out as one of the few innovative efforts undertaken by the GVN and U.S. to cope with a revolutionary, largely political conflict. In a conflict in which mistakes of policy and execution were almost the rule rather than the exception, the so-called "new model" pacification effort of 1967-1970 stands out as at least addressed to the key problems of dealing with rural-based insurgency via techniques that indeed attempted to compensate for the destructiveness of the war. It was a unique wartime expedient, designed specifically to cope with revolutionary war as it had evolved by the late sixties in Vietnam.

III. *Pacification Measurement Systems*

Aside from a handful of in-depth studies of local situations (of which few are based on recent evidence[5]), the most extensive body of available data on the effects (good or bad) of the major 1967-1970 pacification effort lies in the statistical and other reports developed for operational management purposes by the pacifiers themselves. These measurement systems were another notable feature of the "new model" pacification program. Despite their many limitations, the new reporting systems represent a comprehensive attempt at systematic collection and evaluation of relevant pacification data *mostly from the village/hamlet level*—perhaps the most innovative measurement technique of the Vietnam war.

Given the nature of the problem—keeping periodic track of the changing situation in 44 provinces, and 250 districts, over 2000 villages, and over 10,000 hamlets—stress had to be laid on relatively simple quantitative techniques. A similar problem was faced in keeping track of the multitude of small-scale pacification assets—now over 1500 RF companies and 6000 PF platoons, numerous thinly spread national police and RD teams, etc. The systems had to be designed realistically for input by relatively unskilled and overburdened field advisers—since one of the principles adopted was to have all possible inputs made at the lowest feasible level (hamlet if possible)—and then *not* to permit them to be changed as they travelled up the line.

In fact, the most controversial of the pacification measurement systems —the Hamlet Evaluation System (HES), initiated in January 1967—was designed specifically to overcome the flaws inherent in previous, more subjective efforts to assess what was really happening in the countryside. These consisted of largely narrative reports based on Vietnamese sources that had proved consistently overoptimistic. The HES was prepared monthly by U.S. district advisory teams, using a standardized format questionnaire pertaining to physical changes in the hamlet. The HES assessed a matrix of 18 specific security and development indicators according to a simplified five-letter scoring system. At Saigon level, automated data processing is used to save clerical costs and to act as a memory bank.[6]

[5] For example, D. W. P. Elliott and W. A. Stewart, *Pacification and the Viet Cong System in Dinh Tuong: 1966-67*, The RAND Corporation, RM-5788, January 1969. See also Nighswonger, *op. cit.*, on Quang Nam province 1964-1965. Perhaps the most systematic current study of the impact of the war on a sample of 18 villages is the continuing work by S. L. Popkin of Harvard for South East Asia Development Advisory Group (SEADAG) (see below).

[6] See Colonel E.. R. Brigham, "Pacification Measurement," *Military Review*, May 1970, for a short analysis of the HES. He was chief of the CORDS Research and Analysis Division during the evolution.of HES.

As a result, data can be analyzed and compared month by month for the last three and a half years by individual hamlet, village, district, province, region, and SVN as a whole. Functional categories can also be separately analyzed.

HES has been frequently evaluated and criticized by civilian contract analysts; with their help a revised and updated version called HES/70 came into use in 1970 after an extensive trial period. It involves a more detailed and objective uni-dimensional question set, including 25 monthly questions on village/hamlet security and 114 quarterly questions covering all pacification matters. Instead of doing the rating, the adviser simply answers the questions; all scoring is done centrally by a mathematical weighting formula not known to the field. During the 1969 trial period, HES/70 showed consistently lower security ratings (about 4-6 per cent) than the old HES.

CORDS also designed over a dozen specialized data reporting systems, all closely related to each other and to HES for comparative purposes. They include PSDF, *Chieu Hoi*, National Police, Refugee, RD Cadre, and Territorial Forces Management Information Systems, a Pacification Data Bank, Rural Information System, Self-Help Project Monitoring System, Terrorist Incident Reporting System, and the like. Now a system is being designed to help carry out and monitor land reform. Monthly narrative reports on a standard format from U.S. province advisory teams have also been required since 1967; deliberately problem oriented, they provide an additional source of useful insights and were used primarily to identify matters needing attention by higher echelons.

Lest all this seem like too much reporting for its own sake, it should be noted that these systems were designed for management control at each level, not just progress reporting. Consistent emphasis has been placed on problem identification and analysis, not just results. It is impossible to manage a multifaceted pacification program effectively in thousands of villages and hamlets without such reports and measurement systems. But the important point is that these systems provide what one analyst has described as a "gold mine" of raw data on various facets of pacification impact.

In the absence of much else, any assessment of pacification impact must rest heavily on the validity of these CORDS measurement techniques. Much ill-informed criticism has been directed at HES in particular, but most seems to challenge HES for what it does not even claim to be—a measuring of popular attitudes—rather than analyzing it for what it is—a management tool. As with so much involving Vietnam, few critics have taken the time to study what they deplore. Other critics really seem to be complaining less about the HES itself than about the way in which its aggregate scores have often been used in simplistic fashion to advance the notion of "progress." Unfortunately, there is much to this criticism. When HES data is used by officialdom and the media without suitable qualification to claim that "x percent of SVN population is now secure," it is not surprising that such oversimplification sometimes contributes to the Vietnam credibility gap. At any rate, CORDS field briefings on pacification included many relevant qualifiers which were usually ignored in media reporting. Moreover, it is too little recognized that the HES has consistently shown pacification regression and "churning" in rural areas (a fact unduly obscured by use only of overall aggregates). For example, HES provided the only quantifiable and detailed assessment of the sharp drop in rural security following the VC Tet Offensive in 1968.

There are obviously many limitations to the overall utility of pacification measurement system data. Perhaps most significantly, they provide only indirect inferences as to what the population of the countryside really thinks—about the GVN, the VC, security, etc. Periodic physical status indicators are the chief output, first because these are the easiest to measure, and second because of the indispensable need for simplified, standardized procedures if the whole village/hamlet spectrum is to be covered—and with relatively unskilled U.S. advisers as the chief source of input. It is often forgotten that these systems were designed as *U.S.* reporting systems precisely to avoid the kind of overly optimistic Vietnamese reporting which had characterized earlier efforts. For the same reasons, emphasis was placed on generating detailed factual reporting rather than subjective evaluations. While some fudging of figures to show progress has inevitably occurred, particularly when Vietnamese sources are used, a much larger source of perturbation has probably been the frequent shifts in U.S. advisers.

Yet those who have consistently used pacification measurement data have found it generally reliable within its limitations. For example, the analysts in the Systems Analysis Office under the Secretary of Defense have used it regularly for the most impressive "in-house" analytical critiques of pacification performance produced in the last few years. Indeed, one criticism that can be made is not that the mountain of raw data now available is distorted or inaccurate, but that so little of it has yet been analyzed in depth. In a real sense Vietnam has been the most extensively commented on but least solidly analyzed conflict in living memory. Both the establishment and its critics can be faulted on this score. Even CORDS itself places greater stress upon systematic collection of data than upon its exploitation for management purposes. Since most of this data is unclassified, or will doubtless become so, its full exploitation may have to be left to the academic community.

More recently CORDS has been experimenting with poll-type survey techniques, using trained Vietnamese teams to conduct semi-structured interviews of a cross-section sampling of the rural population to determine trends in rural attitudes toward pacification and related subjects. Once this technique is fully developed, and results become available, they should offer useful insights.

IV. *Pacification Impact on Insurgency*

It is still premature to attempt more than an interim assessment of the impact of the "new model" pacification program. Though the improvement of the GVN position in the rural areas since the low point of 1965 is clearly visible, its real depth and extent and its ultimate lasting quality are still untested. But here some important distinctions must be made. First, much more can be inferred about the short-term impact of pacification on the current VC insurgency than about its longer-term effect in helping to create a socio-political environment in which future insurgency would not again flourish.

Second, even over the short-term, it is hard to assess the *relative* extent to which observed changes in the countryside can be properly attributed to the *pacification* program as opposed to other factors. How much is attributable to the shield provided by the allied effort in the "big unit" war, which largely drove the VC/NVA main forces from most populated areas? How much did VC/NVA exhaustion from heavy manpower losses in their 1968 Tet and follow-on offensives weaken the insurgency's rural base? These two factors did much to create the conditions in which the rapid pacification upsurges of late 1968-1970 became possible. Or how much did systematic VC tactics of coercion and terrorism eventually alienate the rural population? How much did factors such as peasant perceptions as to who was winning affect rural actions and attitudes? All such factors undoubtedly had (or will have) some impact. Thus, in an unconventional conflict like Vietnam the relative impact of pacification versus other political, military, or psychological factors is exceedingly hard to sort out.

A third problem is the difficulty of distinguishing between the southern based VC insurgency itself, and North Vietnam's input—especially through NVA infiltration. For analytical purposes at any rate, we cannot dismiss this by calling Vietnam a "civil war." Hanoi's chief contribution in the 1965-1970 period has been well-trained regular forces. Their relative role in proportion to that of the southern VC has steadily increased to the point where over 70 per cent of the VC/NVA main force units and combat support are estimated to be NVA. Vietnam has become more and more "an NVA war" as VC military strength has declined. What began as an externally supported civil war in the south has by now become largely an internally supported "invasion" from the north. Clearly pacification has had much more impact on the faltering VC insurgency than on the NVA main force threat, which could be sustained almost indefinitely by infiltration from the north.

Last is the sheer difficulty previously mentioned of drawing adequate inferences from the mass of statistical data available. It is infinitely easier to quantify the physical changes in the situation in the countryside than to assess the impact of these changes on—to use the once fashionable cliché—the hearts and minds of Vietnam's peasants. In terms of popular reactions, to what extent are any positive effects of pacification (improved security, economic revival, etc.) offset by the negative effects of how the GVN and U.S. have conducted the war? To what extent has coercion, corruption, or arbitrary use of power by GVN administrators taken the bloom off the rose? Is peasant alienation from VC terror and exactions significantly greater than his alienation from similar GVN actions in many cases? Is the farmer fatalistic about all the destruction, or would he rather have a harsh peace even under VC control than the continued destructiveness of the U.S. style of war? One can only pose these questions. No adequate basis for inference is yet available and may never be. But then in what field of analysis are data on behavior and attitudes as satisfactory as those on quantifiable change?

Despite all these caveats, however, at least some tentative inferences can be drawn. In general, the thesis of this article is that the 1967-1970 pacification program probably played a major role in reducing the *VC* insurgency to its present straits. Indeed, the consolidation of GVN local control over the countryside, the consequent drying up of the insurgency's population base and the expansion of the GVN's base, the attrition of the VC politico-administrative apparatus, the large number of ralliers under the *Chieu Hoi* program, and the constructive civil aspects of pacification—restoration of local government autonomy, rural economic revival, local economic and social development—may have contributed as much over the period to damping down the insurgency as the "big unit" casualties inflicted over the same period. The evidence to support this thesis will be assessed under several headings.

Effect on Active Insurgent Strength. The 1967-1970 pacification program has contributed materially to the cumulative attrition of most components of VC active strength. First, the local pacification security forces (principally RF/PF but also the National Police, RD Cadre, and PSDF) have consistently inflicted more casualties on enemy forces—and taken more in return—than ARVN itself. Their activities, as well as their sheer growing presence at the local level, have greatly inhibited VC recruiting, taxation, propaganda, logistics, and even terrorism. Second, the *Chieu Hoi* program has facilitated the rallying of over 160,000 *hoi chanh* ralliers (about two-thirds military) since it began in 1963, and over 132,000 of these came between 1966 and 1970. Though many of these are low-level people, and some no doubt rallied more than once, the cumulative total must have put at least a crimp in VC strength. The great bulk of these ralliers are from III and IV Corps, where the indigenous VC insurgency was largely centered.

Third, even the feeble *Phung Hoang* program has, according to the U.S.-designed reporting system, led to the neutralization of over 40,000 mostly low-level VCI during 1968-1970. Of course, over half of them rallied, were captured, or were killed in the course of military and police operations of one kind or another. But the important point is that the growing if belated focus on neutralizing the VC politico-military apparatus as well as insurgent military strength has probably seriously reduced insurgent capabilities. The most recently published figures indicate that the remaining VCI are now carried at about 70,000.[7]

Whether or not the above figures are wholly accurate, the point is that the cumulative impact of these pacification programs has contributed materially to the reduction of insurgent strength to a point where, without continued infusion of NVA personnel (and now reportedly political cadre), most professional observers estimate that it would be difficult for the VC insurgency to survive as a major threat to the GVN.

The fact that the VC are increasingly targeting pacification programs may be an interesting indicator of the extent to which pacification is hurting the VC. During the three day April 1970 offensive "high point," for example, nearly half of the enemy attacks were against pacification targets.

[7] George McArthur, *Los Angeles Times,* Part I, April 2, 1970, p. 4.

Recent VC documents clearly indicate greater 1970 concern over pacification and direct greater efforts to combat it. Of course, all this may be partly because harassing pacification is a cheap way to keep the pot boiling during a "protracted war" phase.

Effect on Insurgent Population Base. Pacification programs, in conjunction with other factors, have had a similar effect on the VC-controlled rural population base. This can be systematically measured by the HES, which, with due allowance for the necessary qualifications, nonetheless is better than any other data for measuring such trends. It has been officially admitted that at the end of 1964, only 40 per cent of South Vietnam's population was under government "control"—a sometime thing in those days—and over 20 per cent under VC control. Even when HES was first instituted in January 1967, only some 62.1 per cent of a total 16.3 million people were then rated as even "relatively secure," some 18.5 per cent as contested, and still 19.4 per cent as admittedly VC-controlled. Furthermore, a high percentage of this increase in "relatively secure" population in 1965-1967 did not occur because of increased security in the countryside, but rather as a result of refugee movements and the accelerated urbanization taking place. However, these factors can be removed from the calculation by considering only *rural* HES scores. In January 1967, only some 46.3 per cent of the *rural* population was rated as relatively secure. Even at the end of 1967 less than 50 per cent of the rural population was so rated, and this dropped further as a result of the 1968 Tet Offensive, which was faithfully reflected in the HES. But the June 1970 figures (from the revised HES/70, which is much more sensitive to enemy activity and VCI presence) rate over 91 per cent of SVN's 17.9 million population as "relatively secure," 7.2 per cent as contested, and only 1.4 per cent or 256,000 rural people as VC-controlled. The great bulk of this VC-controlled population is concentrated in less than a dozen of the 44 provinces. The 1969-1970 gains have been mostly in the key rural areas.

Whatever one's prejudices as to the precision of these figures, there is little doubt that GVN domination of the countryside has expanded rapidly since late 1968 at the expense of the VC-controlled population base, with inevitable effects on VC recruiting capabilities. Of course, GVN general mobilization in 1968, which led to the build-up of RVNAF and para-military forces to over 1.2 million men, has also operated to sop up manpower which might otherwise be available to the VC.

Effect on Rural Security. A mass of quantitative data, mostly from the hamlet/village level, in the HES and other data banks provides overwhelming evidence that the physical security provided the bulk of the rural population has expanded considerably since the 1965 low point. HES *security* scores for *rural* population show an increase in relative security (ABC categories) to 90.5 per cent at end-1969. For those who are unwilling to accept so-called "C" hamlets as even relatively secure, even A and B population has risen to about 75 per cent as of June 1970.

Increased security in most populated areas, though still spotty in some cases, is also amply evident to the observer. There is also a direct correlation between increases in local GVN security forces and the resulting improvement in security indices. Improved security can also be directly inferred from the decline in the overall *incident rate*. From available statistics it is clear that the number of battalion-sized attacks and even lesser incidents was down significantly in 1969 from 1968 and has declined even further in 1970. Terrorism is still high, especially in March through May of 1970, but the overall terror, sabotage, etc. trend is down from 1968 to 1970. It is worth repeating, however, that the overall decline in the intensity of the war can be attributed to many other factors besides pacification.

Equally significant, *the war has become largely localized*. Analysis of the 1970 incident rate and the HES statistics show clearly that both the military war and terrorism now impact mostly on a few key areas. Leaving aside the "big unit" war in the almost unpopulated jungle and mountain areas along the borders, insurgency-type activity or VC incursions into populated areas are largely concentrated in the three provinces of southern I Corps, Quang Nam, Quang Tin, and Quang Ngai; Binh Dinh, Phu Yen, Pleiku, and Kontum in northern II Corps; and four provinces in the Delta, Kien Hoa, Vinh Binh, An Xuyen, and Kien Giang (the last mostly because it is along the border). In most populated areas of the other 33 provinces, the intensity of conflict and even terrorism has radically declined—in many cases to sporadic harassment.

The number of refugees who are increasingly returning to the countryside (with help from the GVN refugee resettlement program) is another gross indicator of improved rural security. Excluding refugees from Cambodia, the number on the rolls has declined from over two million at the highest point to some 1.5 million in February 1969, and then to around 217,000 by mid-1970. While refugee statistics (especially earlier ones) are not wholly reliable, they are sufficiently reliable to establish this broad trend. The return to villages has continued in 1970.

Effect on Rural Participation in GVN-Sponsored Activities. It is at least partly relevant that popular participation in GVN programs, organizations, and activities of one sort or another has soared in recent years. No doubt to some extent this is a function of GVN pressure or coercion, or at least a matter of the peasant doing what he is told to do. Moreover, such participation does not necessarily equate with active commitment, though it would be equally mistaken to argue that it has no such meaning at all. At any rate, the rural population is becoming heavily engaged in the business of local government, local defense, self-help, etc., particularly since the Tet Offensive of 1968. Significant on this score are the rapid increases of GVN military and paramilitary forces (excluding PSDF) from 700,000 in April 1968 to about 1.2 million men today, and the rising enrollment in the part-time Popular Self-Defense Force, all since May, 1968, to between 3 and 3.5 million (though in urban as well as rural areas).

Increased *popular participation in GVN-sponsored elections* also may be relevant to popular acquiescence in the governmental process. While there has unquestionably been some fudging of the results in local cases, the extensive statistics available since 1967 on voter registration, participation, and number of candidates are considered generally reliable by professional observers in the field. In May 1965, only 3.8 million (of 4.2 million registered voters) voted in the provincial and municipal elections. In September 1966, 4.3 million of 5.2 million voted for the Constituent Assembly. The proportion of the 5.87 million registered voters voting in the 1967 national elections was 83 per cent. The proportion voting in the 1970 provincial and municipal council elections of 28 June 1970 dropped to 72.5 per cent (as usually happens in local vs. national elections), but the number of registered voters had risen to 6.1 million. The number of candidates for each seat (3.5 in the 1970 elections) has also increased. New faces are much in evidence; in I Corps the number of new candidates who won in village/hamlet elections increased from 20 per cent in 1969 to 30 per cent in 1970. The 1970 provincial and municipal council elections in I Corps produced 60 per cent new faces since 1967. At the lowest level some 961 villages and 5344 hamlets *elected* local administrations in 1969, bringing total elected local governments to 2048 out of 2151 villages and 9849 out of 10,496 hamlets. Some of these local elections were only nominal, but given the sheer looseness and inefficiency of the GVN at all levels, few would contend that local elections were mostly rigged. While difficult as yet to evaluate, the GVN's continuing efforts to restore local autonomy at the grass roots level have apparently stimulated greater rural popular interest in local government.

Effect on Socio-Economic Conditions in the Countryside. Here again, mostly quantitative indices must be relied upon. It is difficult to translate into meaningful impact all the USAID-type statistics on hamlet or other schools built, teachers trained, fertilizer distributed, rural dispensaries and province hospitals constructed, refugees cared for, wells dug, roads and waterways opened and repaired, tractors imported, markets built, self-help projects completed, or piasters and dollars spent. But there is little question that the range of services and assistance provided the rural population in GVN-controlled areas, mostly through the pacification program, has increased dramatically by 1969-1970 over 1965-1967. The net impact of priority measures to revive the rural economy has been to reverse the long decline in agricultural production, and according to a recent U.S. economic study, to make many Delta farmers the "new rich" of Vietnam. By June 1970 there were an estimated 3400 tractors in the Delta (IV Corps), a doubling over fifteen months as a result of agricultural development loans and sheer private spending. Of course, increased agricultural income is far from evenly distributed, and against all the improvement must be weighed the continued difficulties posed by military operations, GVN inefficiency, corruption, and the like.

Effect on Rural Attitudes Toward VC and GVN. So far this tentative analysis of pacification impact has stressed mostly quantifiable factors. It is far harder to assess systematically the effect on rural attitudes and commitment to the contending sides. Yet even here *there is a growing body of evidence that the farmers are turning against the VC*, even though they may not look with favor on the GVN. The decline in VC popular support has been noted by many observers, and attributed to a variety of causes. It can also be documented in numerous rallier interviews. Some point to how increased VC use of coercion, forced conscription, high taxation, and terror have alienated farmers in many areas. Statistics indicate that more than three-fourths of the terrorist victims in the period 1967-1970 were ordinary civilians. The widespread destruction in the Tet and May Offensives of 1968 generated a particularly noticeable anti-VC backlash. Others point to a drastic decline in the appeal to peasants of life in VC-controlled areas, as opposed to materially improved conditions in areas under GVN domination. Still others contend that the farmers are increasingly coming to believe that the GVN is winning, and in pragmatic fashion are gravitating toward the side that has the "mandate of heaven."

But in terms of generating positive rural political support for the GVN, the evidence is much more spotty. And this may be the heart of the matter. To Popkin, one of the few scholars who has addressed this issue, "the central problem of pacification is how to translate economic resources and military power into village control." He sees this as "a political and not a technical problem,"[8] and renders the tentative verdict, based on 1966-1967 and 1969 field observations, that:

> In the term's most common meaning–physical security, governmental presence and economic benefits–most of South Vietnam is pacified. But this only means that the concept has always been inadequate, for peasants that have endured decades of mobilization and brutalization are no longer necessarily willing to act as passive subjects to be ruled from afar.[9]

In effect Popkin sees pacification as succeeding in its proximate aims but by no means yet achieving positive rural political support for the GVN. He recognizes that the Thieu regime is attempting to build a rural political base through methods already described. But to him:

> Saigon's problem has always been the lack of positive support even though there is often resentment or mistrust of the Viet Cong. And until positive links are made with the peasant population, until they identify with and feel represented by the government in Saigon, the risk of a Viet Cong comeback will remain.[10]

He grants that the new pacification programs in the village "have begun to energize a long dormant village political structure," but sees Thieu as hemmed in in his attempts to move further in this direction by the ARVN, which regards its still dominant role in rural administration as a base of political power which it will be reluctant to relinquish.

> What support Thieu may get from the people is likely to be irrelevant unless ARVN is reformed. For the essence of the conflict is not between a traditional peasant and a modernizing state but between a newly modern, politically sensitive peasantry and a state that is jealous of its own power and prerogatives.[11]

Popkin's critique, based on actual field research in 18 villages, is perhaps the most perceptive and up-to-date yet available. Yet to what extent should a wartime program like pacification be measured in terms of what must essentially be a longer-term political process lasting perhaps a de-

[8] Popkin, SEADAG Discussion Paper, "Village Authority Patterns in Vietnam," *Asia* (2 June 1969), p. 1.

[9] Popkin, "Pacification: Politics and the Village," *Asian Survey*, (August 1970), p. 663.

[10] *Ibid.*, p. 664.

[11] Popkin, *ibid.* The author's own observations in Vietnam, 7-19 July 1970, would tend at least partially to confirm his thesis of the growing clash of interest between elected village councils and the military province and especially district chiefs who are reluctant to share local power.

cade? It seems too much to expect that in only three years or so even the major pacification effort finally launched in Vietnam should have achieved more than the restoration of relative local security in most areas, a considerable degree of economic revival, and the re-establishment of at least a semblance of popularly based local administration—with a substantial degree of popular acquiesence and perhaps some support. Thus, Popkin's verdict seems a bit premature. If pacification is looked on as mainly aimed at suppressing insurgency and creating a climate within which the longer-term political process can have its inning, then Vietnam pacification may have been (as indeed Popkin grants) largely successful.[12] It has bought time to let the GVN see if it can knit together the government and the peasantry. At a minimum the peasantry now apparently sees a brighter future under the GVN than under the Viet Cong, aside from regarding the GVN as now having the "mandate of heaven." Moreover, more recent 1970 rural attitude surveys (by Vietnamese) show a more positive rural attitude toward the GVN than Popkin has suggested.

Indeed, Popkin himself sees the conflict which will now determine ultimate GVN viability as one between the peasantry and ARVN rather than between the GVN and VC. Other observers would rate the ARVN's political power as less of a fearsome threat to Thieu. In a real sense he has more control over ARVN than anyone else, a result of his powers to promote and reward as the senior general and president. In any case, ARVN is not very cohesive as a political power center and is increasingly being redeployed toward the borders, away from populated areas.

Moreover, the decentralization of power has gone further than Popkin suggests. Some 70,000 village/hamlet officials have been educated at the Vung Tau National Training Center for their new responsibilities (and harangued by Thieu himself to exercise them). Greater decentralization has occurred in 1970 (e.g., autonomous village budgets, new provincial councils) and more is planned for 1971 (e.g., election of province chiefs as called for in the 1967 constitution). Though local autonomy still exists

[12] For a view that the extent of popular support for a government, or its shift from an insurgency to a government, is *not* a reliable indicator of success, see Nathan Leites and Charles Wolf, Jr., *Rebellion and Authority* (Chicago: Markham, 1970), pp. 87-89, reviewed in this issue of the *Journal*. Theirs is the only systematic analysis of indicators of success in counter-insurgency known to the author. In their view, the "hearts and minds" theory that popular attitudes play a decisive role in enabling insurgencies to achieve success is grossly overdrawn. They see popular behavior as depending "not only on likes and dislikes" but also on the opportunities and costs to the population of choosing whether to follow their attitudinal preferences. Moreover, to them "the progress made by each side in an insurgency influences the affiliations of most of the population as much as, or more than, it is influenced by those affiliations." (pp. 150-151)

more on paper than in reality in many areas, and a natural conflict of interest is emerging between the new village leaders and the military men who dominate at the district and province levels, the trend is in the right direction.

If Thieu survives, he will almost certainly push decentralization further for his own political purposes. Moreover, despite the natural conflict of interest between ARVN and the newly emerging rural groups, there is less of a conflict inherent in the relations between these groups and the central government. It is easier to envisage a sharing of power between the village at the local level and the GVN at the center than between local civilians and military leadership groups. In any case, the related diffusion of power now taking place between the executive, legislative, and judicial branches will operate to limit the impositions of the center on the village. Neither Thieu nor ARVN are any longer as much the free agents they used to be.

V. *Tentative Conclusion*

In sum, the gathering weight of recent evidence indicates that the 1967-1970 "new model" pacification program, with all its flaws and weaknesses, has contributed materially to at least a short-run improvement in the GVN's ability to cope with rural insurgency. There is no doubt that the position of the GVN vis-a-vis the VC in the countryside has grown much stronger—militarily, economically, and administratively—since 1965-1966. The dramatic physical improvements in most areas are highly visible, and the trends are further confirmed by the systematic CORDS measurement systems, despite their limitations. The weight of evidence also shows that the VC position has drastically declined in all areas of Vietnam and remains a major threat in only about 8-12 provinces. Moreover, despite U.S. withdrawals, GVN capabilities to push the pacification process further still appear to be growing, and the capabilities of the southern VC (though not necessarily the NVA) appear to be on the wane.

It should also be borne in mind that pacification's contribution to these results was achieved via programs that have been primarily Vietnamese staffed and run from the outset, though extensively subsidized and logistically supported by the U.S. Even so, the direct U.S. dollar input to pacification in probably the peak year 1970 is only about $777 million out of the many billions still being spent, which makes pacification probably more cost-effective than most major wartime programs in Vietnam. Nor have pacification programs generally entailed the sort of counterproductive side effects on rural attitudes characteristic of many aspects of the "big unit" war. Indeed, many programs (refugee aid, village development and self-help, etc.) were designed partly to compensate for these.

What is less apparent, and far less subject to measurement, is how lasting the change in the countryside or the degree of positive rural commitment is to a still feeble GVN. In the author's view, the war and its consequences (e.g., pacification) have stimulated *what amounts to a rural revolution in Vietnam*—politically, socially, and economically. But the extent to which this revolution will benefit the GVN's cause over time is still unclear. Definitive evidence may not be available for years. Moreover, the VC—though greatly weakened—is still a force to be reckoned with. Indeed, despite the growing evidence as to pacification's short-term impact on rural insurgency, such other factors as new NVA offensives, political changes in Saigon, or the terms of a negotiated settlement may so affect the final outcome in Vietnam that no real test of pacification's ultimate impact may ever be feasible.

EPILOGUE

About a year ago when writing the above article I cited the great lack of informed public coverage of pacification in the 1967-70 period, and how most commentaries on it seemed to be unduly influenced by the growing controversy about our ill-fated intervention itself. This situation has grown worse, and in the strained atmosphere of today, dispassionate analysis is even more notable by its absence. Little attempt is made to buttress sweeping generalizations with even a modicum of fact. Pejorative condemnation tends to crowd out rational analysis.

Who can question the legitimacy of academic controversy over the causes and consequences of America's disastrous experience in Vietnam? These deserve to be fully aired and debated. If there were war crimes (in a generally accepted sense, if one exists), let these too be fully aired. But it does this debate no service when dissent slops over into *ad hominem* insinuations which demean the debate and the debaters and which substitute polemic for evidence.

In this category lies the charge, made elsewhere in this volume, that in the view of knowledgeable observers I deserve trial as a war criminal, presumably because of my role in the so-called "new model" pacification program which I helped develop in 1966-68. I am unaware of any *qualified* observers who have made this charge and can only conclude that pacification has been lumped with all the rest that the U.S. did or supposedly did in Vietnam as a subject for blanket condemnation. To anyone familiar with the post-1966 program, such charges of guilt by association must seem strange.

Some have urged me to shrug off such nonsense and not to dignify it by rebuttal. Others have rightly pointed out that anything I write will inevitably be seen by many as a self-serving apologia. I have decided to pay this price. In my experience, government officials tend to be not only too secretive about their purposes and actions, but too reluctant to rebut criticism even when it wholly lacks validity. This is hardly the way to stimulate informed dialogue between government and its critics, to the benefit of those it serves.

Hence this note to the reader. I am fully prepared to assume my share of responsibility for anything I did or anything that was done by the advisory organization I headed. In retrospect, we made many mistakes. But I am unaware of any criminal acts by any definition for which we should stand accountable. Let anyone produce even respectable allegations that we did.

Of course I did hold a responsible senior position from April, 1966 through April, 1967 as Special Assistant to the President for what was termed "the Other War" in Vietnam. It was essentially a nation-building effort, an attempt to help build a viable socioeconomic fabric in the middle of a shooting war. Most activities I oversaw in that capacity are on the public record in the so-called Komer Report on The Other War, released by the White House in September 1966.

From May, 1967 to November, 1968 I served in Vietnam as chief pacification adviser to the GVN. My role, and that of the organization I helped create, was to provide advice and logistic/financial help to the GVN's own revivified pacification effort. *This program,* in glaring contrast to the "big unit war," *was wholly Vietnamese manned and commanded.* We and they both wanted it this way. As a matter of policy we decided that Americans could not and should not perform this role. We Americans helped shape it and vigorously supported it. But an essential strength of pacification was precisely that it *was* a Vietnamese, not an American, program—whatever costs this entailed. And all things considered, it has proved a reasonably effective one to date. It shows that the GVN could finally put together a response to revolutionary war that was predominantly constructive rather than destructive. To me, it deserves far more credit than blame.

The record of U.S. pacification support and advice need not be hidden behind a classified screen. As those from the media who dealt with us during 1966-68 well realize, we in CORDS, and I personally, were about as candid, forthright, accessible, and responsive as anyone in Vietnam could be. We had nothing to hide. If our record is not clear, it is more because pacification and the "Other War" did not seem good copy than that we were evasive or dissimulating. Some might see me in particular as guilty of the "crime" of over-optimism, but I in turn see them as failing to analyze thoroughly before pinning on such cozy labels of convenience.

The brief description of the post-1967 pacification effort in my article shows that, as practiced since 1966, it was close to the antithesis of any approach stressing attrition by technological means. Far from seeking totalitarian controls over the population, the stress was on local self-government, political checks and balances, and rule of law. Far from seeking the displacement and dispossession of the rural population, the pacifiers (abandoning the Strategic Hamlet Regroupment approach), objected repeatedly to population relocation for military reasons and sought continuously to improve the social and economic lot of the farmers. Far from "generating" refugees, the pacifiers sought to minimize such harsh military measures; we were the ones who took care of refugees, not those who created them. Far from relying on bombing, napalm, defoliation, and other technological means, the pacification platoons and companies—recruited from the countryside—had no weapons larger than mortars and served to protect the villages from enemy attack. It is simply loose thinking to confuse pacification with the "big unit war."

In the year since my article was written, pacification has become even more civilianized, as the shooting war continues to wind down. Over 500,000 acres have recently been distributed to farmers under the 1970 land reform law. The rural economy is booming in most areas. Provincial Councils have been elected. Far more refugees seem to be returning to their villages or resettling than are being created anew. All this despite the accelerating U.S. withdrawal, which further strengthens the hypothesis that the GVN has finally captured the nationalist revolution from the Viet Cong, and that what is still going on in Vietnam today is a quasi-conventional war pitting the North against the South.

Like most programs in Vietnam, the so-called "new model" pacification program had its weaknesses. There was too much corruption, inefficiency, poor local leadership, and the like. Some critics point to the GVN *Phung Hoang* program, designed to combat the clandestine Viet Cong politico/administrative/logistic/terror apparatus, as being often misused by GVN officials for other purposes. But the record will show that the chief critics were the U.S. advisers themselves. Indeed, senior GVN pacification officials and U.S. advisers probably made a greater effort to correct excesses and to remove venal or incompetent officials than in most other facets of the Vietnam war. Nor can such excesses be isolated from the context in which they were committed. They largely reflect the problems of a half-formed government and society under the stress of revolutionary war. It is doublethink to argue otherwise.

In sum, it is regrettable that I should have to rebut such uninformed allegations against one of the more sensible and constructive endeavors which the U.S. belatedly supported in Vietnam. This is the first time, to my knowledge, that such assertions have been made. Given the temper of the time, however, it will probably not be the last. So I prefer dealing with them now. One price of the Vietnam tragedy is the deep scars it has inflicted on the American psyche. I can only hope that responsible academic circles will resist the temptation to let pejorative allegation masquerade as reality, and will insist on temperate analysis. Only in this way will we ever learn the why and how of one of the most tragic chapters in America's role in the world.

June 23, 1971 R. W. Komer

JEAN BAECHLER

Revolutionary and Counter-Revolutionary War: Some Political and Strategic Lessons from the First Indochina War and Algeria

As is true of all discrete historical occurrences, the French experiences with revolutionary war in Indochina and in Algeria have their own uniqueness.[1] These wars, however, also illustrate well-known, generally applicable maxims systematized by Clausewitz. Three of his concepts appear particularly relevant to our analysis of revolutionary war:

[1] There is an extensive bibliography for the two wars: Yves Courrière, *La Guerre d'Algérie:* Volume I, *Les Fils de la Toussaint* (Paris: Fayard, 1968); Volume II, *Le Temps des Leopards* (1969); Volume III, *L'Heure des Colonels* (1970). I have consulted the following sources for Viet Minh accounts: Nguyen Giap, *L'Armée Populaire de Liberation du Viet Nam* (Hanoi, 1952); *Dien Bien Phu* (Hanoi, 1959); *Guerre du Peuple, Armée du Peuple* (Hanoi, 1961). For the French point of view: M. Bigeard, *Contre-Guerrilla* (Algiers: Bacconnier, n.d.); L. Bodard, *La Guerre d'Indochine*, 3 volumes, (Paris: Gallimard, n.d.); G. Bonnet, *Les Guerres Insurrectionelles et Révolutionnaires* (Paris: Payot, 1958); Bernard Fall, *Guerres d'Indochine* (Paris: Robert Laffont, 1970); P. Langlais, *Dien Bien Phu* (Paris: Empire, 1963); P. Rolland, *Contre Guerrilla* (Paris: Louvois, 1956); J. Roy, *La Bataille de Dien Bien Phu* (Paris: Juilliard, 1963); and R. Trinquier, *La Guerre Moderne* (Paris: Table Ronde, 1961).

Professor Jean Baechler received his agregé at the University of Paris in history in 1962. In 1966 he joined the National Scientific Research Center (Sociological Section). His principal publications include: *The Politics of Trotsky* (Paris: Armand Colin, 1968) and *Revolutionary Phenomena* (Paris: Universities of France Press, 1970).

1. War is a duel between two protagonists, *but* within each camp one must distinguish three levels of interaction: the combatant forces, the domestic politics of the antagonists, and the actions and reactions of the international community. This distinction means that political dynamics are much more operative in revolutionary wars than in classical conventional wars.
2. There are two grand strategies possible: the attack, which aims at winning the war; and the defense, which seeks not to lose it. In revolutionary war, the defense enjoys a decisive superiority over the attack.
3. War is the continuation of policy by other means; and one must carefully distinguish the political end from the military objective. In revolutionary wars especially, the political goal must *always* determine the military objective.

Revolutionary wars, in contrast to classical conventional wars, are wholly social phenomena, and analysis requires some consideration of the social systems of the antagonists. As in all wars, the strategies of the antagonists are dialectically linked; the strategy of the one determines that of the other. Because of the three levels of interaction, however, the revolutionary battlefield is much more complex. Yet, the most persistent error of the French authorities in the field was to disregard the strategy of the other side, or worse, to sneer at it. The purpose of this article is to analyze the military and political strategies of the insurgents and of the established authorities. We will begin with the insurrection, for it is the insurrection which decides the stakes of war and establishes the ground rules of the struggle.

I. *Insurrection: The Political Goals*

The quest for sovereignty. The quest for sovereignty and legitimacy is the logical cause and end of the whole insurrectional movement. Indeed, the mainspring of the process of decolonization has been the will to reconquer or to define a national or ethnic identity. Such an identity, however, is only guaranteed from the moment the former colony has the advantage of a full and complete sovereignty. Internally, sovereignty is defined by the possibility of establishing a legitimate political, economic, and social system without foreign interference; and externally, by the possibility of freely choosing a place in the international system. Whatever the initial level of demands—equal rights with the French, internal autonomy, independence with special ties, or total independence—and regardless of whether the mother country yields to or represses these demands with force, the quest for sovereignty is inevitable. Therefore, it is wrong to believe that the eventual fulfillment of certain Indochinese or (especially) Algerian demands would have enabled the French to keep these people under their control. It is certain that these colonies would have achieved sovereignty anyway.

The pursuit of sovereignty in no way prejudices the nature of the socio-political system that will be set up, or the international alignment of the new political unit. The choices are open, and consequently are determined by other factors. The principal factor is war itself; what is probable is that the longer and harsher the war, the more *extremist* the regime which will finally take over from the colonialists.

The conquest of the people. At best, conquest of the people will result in the active support, at worst in the neutrality, of most of the population. This conquest is a technical necessity imposed by the initial disproportion of the contending forces. Lest they perish from logistical asphyxiation or be limited to sporadic blows, the insurgents must be able to rely on the complicity of the majority of the people and the rallying of activists. The neutrality of the population poses no problem. Aside from minorities and the assimilated (for example, the Algerian veterans of the two world wars and the Algerian and Indochinese social strata which were completely Francophile), the population constitutes a source of implicit support for the insurgents.

Indeed, even if we were to suppose that a population could ever be induced to identify with its conqueror, French colonialization was too short and too superficial to achieve this empathy. Consciousness of the difference of the Other and of his menacing character never fades away. The intermittent reappearance of insurrections from the earliest days of colonization proves that colonization is the imposition of an order which is essentially unstable. As a result, the apparent neutrality of the population has every chance of transforming itself into active support from the moment the insurgents successfully convince the people that they are able to win. From this point on, revolutionary vocations will multiply (especially among the youth and students) and a snowball phenomenon of activism will occur. Participation in the liberation movement begins in the ranks of the elite inherited from the old regime as well as in the ranks of the new elite born from contact with the West. Together these elites suffer most directly from the limitations of colonialization; but are in the best position to determine opportunities to construct a strategy for liberation.

The mobilization of the masses—composed essentially of the traditional peasantry—poses more difficult problems. With important exceptions, for example on the plantations, the masses do not suffer directly from colonialization. On the contrary, the masses were probably dissatisfied with the prevailing order even before colonialization. This is particularly valid in reference to Indochina where the political and social system rested on the subjugation and exploitation of an overabundant and miserable peasantry. The insurgents are therefore confronted with the enormous task of convincing the masses that the struggle is social as well as national. And for the peasantry social combat means a struggle for land. This is why the essential point of the insurgents' program is agrarian land reform, and why a war for national liberation necessarily becomes a revolutionary war.

Armed insurrection is constantly accompanied by intense *political* agitation among the masses, with all that this signifies: a deepening of social cleavages in the countryside, violent elimination of opponents, rigorous mobilization of the population by activists, and—where the absence of the colonialists allows it—the setting up of a politico-administrative infrastructure that foreshadows the future regime and competes with the incumbents for political legitimacy and control of the people. These activities, however, lead directly to a fundamental socio-political choice which has divisive repercussions among the leaders of the insurrection. Indeed, as long as the goal is simply national independence, unanimity can exist. From the moment the insurgent program adopts political and social aims, ideological and social cleavages will appear and threaten unity. This in turn provides the colonial authorities with the possibility of exploiting these divisions and of trying to gain the support of the most acceptable factions. A group of loyalist ralliers will form, composed for the most part of men who have everything to fear from a social revolution and who will resist any attempt by the insurgents or by the established authorities to impose a social upheaval aimed at mobilizing the masses. Struggles among rebel factions and the settling of accounts among the insurgents will also take place. It is very likely that in this struggle the extremists will finally triumph and consequently a radicalization of the insurgent movement will take place. This dialectical result is obviously not endogenous, but is entirely determined by the reactions of the established authorities. The longer and harsher the war, the more the consequences of this radicalization reveal themselves.

The international environment. The Indochinese and Algerian insurgents benefited from direct and indirect outside support, both of which were equally important. Direct help was provided by the bordering countries, China on the one hand, Morocco and especially Tunisia on the other. The insurgents had the opportunity of establishing bases outside the country in order to train, regroup, and form units. They also received, through their sanctuary bases, arms and logistical support which would come from all over the world.[2] Indirect support is more subtle and entails, broadly speaking, two strategies. First, it is necessary to insert a wedge between the mother country and its allies. This can be done by convincing them of the illegitimacy of the counter-revolutionary war or by showing them that its pursuit can lead to issues which threaten the international balance of power.[3] Second, it is necessary to alert international public opinion so that its awakening might bring pressure to bear on the adversary: no country, especially a democratic one, can indefinitely neglect the condemnation of world public opinion. For example, the main objective of the blind and bloody attacks in Algiers in 1955-56 was to publicize the existence of the Algerian revolution. An attack carried out in the center of the city of Algiers had a far greater repercussion than a successful ambush deep in the Aures region. Most international public opinion is essentially anti-colonialist; but even if it were not, the natural tendency is to side with the underdog.

The insurrection aims at a clear and simple end toward which it is possible to channel all energies and around which one can hope to rally world opinion. The clarity of the political goal is essential for it is politics which determine the outcome of the war; a bad or imprecise policy results in an unsuccessful war. As Clausewitz has stated:

> ... under all circumstances War is to be regarded not as an independent thing, but as a political instrument; and it is only by taking this point of view that we can avoid finding ourselves in opposition to all military history.... Now, the first, the grandest, and most decisive act of judgment which the Statesman and General exercises is rightly to understand ... the War in which he engages and not to take it for something, or to wish to make of it something, which by the nature of its

[2] To have a powerful and active ally on one's doorstep is essential. Indeed it enables one to avoid asphyxiation and poses the problem for the established authorities of whether to expand the conflict. The French army set up between Tunisia and Algeria an extremely effective barrier, but this did not prevent the insurrection from spreading.

[3] The first argument was used by Ho Chi Minh with the Americans; for many years, the Americans were convinced that France was engaged in the criminal attempt to keep Indochina within the French Empire. The second argument convinced the Americans that the Algerian War would lead to the Sovietization of the Maghreb.

> relations it is impossible for it to be. This is, therefore, the first, the most comprehensive, of all strategic questions.[4]

This advice applies to both antagonists, but the insurgents in their exploitation of political advantages establish the ground rules which determine the nature of the revolutionary war.

II. *Insurrection: The Military Strategy*

The center of gravity of the enemy. The goal of military operations is to disarm the enemy; this is accomplished (materially and/or morally) when his center of gravity is destroyed. The center of gravity varies according to the political regime involved and the type of war. According to Clausewitz,

> Alexander had his centre of gravity in his Army, as had Gustavus Adolphus, Charles XII, and Frederick the Great, and the career of any-one of them would soon have been brought to a close by the destruction of his fighting force: in States torn by internal dissensions, this centre generally lies in the capital; in small States dependent on greater ones, it lies generally in the Army of these allies; in a confederacy, it lies in the unity of interests; in a national insurrection, in the person of the chief leader, and in public opinion. Against these points the blow must be directed.[5]

In a revolutionary war, the counter-insurgent's center, in these cases that of the French, *is not* the expeditionary force. Indeed, in a revolutionary war the disproportion of forces in favor of the established authorities is such that the destruction of the expeditionary corps is almost impossible. But in the unlikely event that this were to happen, it would mean that one type of war had been lost: it would still be possible to start another one with new forces from the mother country.[6] France has never waged total war even in Algeria. An expeditionary corps, which represented only a small proportion of the mobilizable armed forces, was always used.

It is clear that the center of gravity of the counter-insurgent lies in the mother country and more precisely in the national will to fight. In a

[4] Clausewitz, *On War* (London: Pelican Books, 1968), edited by Anatol Rapoport, p. 121.

[5] *Ibid.*, p. 389.

[6] Dien Bien Phu was an absurdity from all points of view—especially on the political level for it meant a double or nothing situation. Thus defeat meant the loss of North Vietnam through a war fought by a limited number of professionals and volunteers who did not have the moral support of the mother country. A national awakening to the situation would have been expressed by a massive dispatchment of troops and the start of a new war.

pluralistic political system there is inevitably, however, a party in favor of negotiation and peace. Consequently, the prime strategy of the insurgents is to try to turn this party into a majority. In order to accomplish this, the insurgents must hold out militarily long enough for war-weariness to develop in the mother country, or else they must inflict enough casualties so that the costs incurred seem disproportionate to the stakes. Using systematic propaganda to take advantage of the natural divisiveness inherent in pluralistic polities, the insurgents must convince a majority in the mother country that two nations are not struggling, but rather that an aspiring nation is resisting an imperialist war faction in the mother country. An appropriate measure is the refusal to bring terrorism into the mother country, for this would then result in the defeat of the peace party. The Algerian F.L.N. found it difficult to accept this principle; some wanted to put France to fire and sword with the help of immigrant workers. There were, for example, several spectacular attacks against the oil installations in Marseilles. Of course, these incidents turned people almost unanimously *against* the F.L.N.

In the case of a non-hegemonial power like France, its allies represent a secondary center of gravity. The insurgents strive to erode alliance support or transform it into opposition. They can accomplish this by carefully avoiding interference with the interests of the allies and by using diplomatic blackmail.

The strategy of defense, or the prevention of defeat. Because of its initial matériel and numerical inferiority, the insurrection must assume a strategic defensive posture to shield itself and conserve its offensive capability. As Clausewitz has noted, strategic defense does not mean mere passivity, but a shrewd attempt to extend the offense spatially and temporally:

> The idea of wearing out the enemy in a struggle amounts in practice to *a gradual exhaustion of the physical powers and of the will by the long continuance of exertion.*
>
> Now, if we want to overcome the enemy by the duration of the contest, we must content ourselves with as small objects as possible, for it is in the nature of the thing that a great end requires a greater expenditure of force than a small one; but the smallest object that we can propose to ourselves is simple passive resistance, that is a combat without any positive view. In this way, therefore, our means attain their greatest relative value, and therefore the result is best secured. How far now can this negative mode of proceeding be carried? Plain-

> ly not to absolute passivity, for mere endurance would not be fighting; and the defensive is an activity by which so much of the enemy's power must be destroyed that he must give up his object. . . . If then the negative purpose, that is the concentration of all the means into a state of pure resistance, affords a superiority in the contest, and if this advantage is enough to *balance* whatever superiority in numbers the adversary may have, then the mere *duration* of the contest will suffice gradually to bring the loss of force on the part of the adversary to a point at which the political object can no longer be an equivalent, a point at which, therefore, he must give up the contest. We see then that this class of means, the wearing out of the enemy, includes the great number of cases in which the weaker resists the stronger.[7]

This defensive strategy of revolutionary war corresponds to several simple maxims of guaranteed efficacy. First, never accept combat with an enemy attacking in force, but retreat before superior force. To illustrate this point one can cite the example in Indochina of the offensive along la Route Coloniale No. 4, along the Chinese border in 1949, or the Battle of the Black River and Hoa Binh (November 14, 1951–February 24, 1952). Any offensive necessarily reaches a climax after which time plays against the attacker: he must administer occupied territory, disperse his troops, and maintain logistics lines; or the attacker must retreat and risk ambush. The evacuation of the garrison at Cao Bang on la Route Coloniale No. 4, (October, 1951) became a disaster. Second, attack only when assured of an absolute superiority. This maxim presupposes that the counter-insurgent has dispersed his forces and that the insurgents can concentrate forces rapidly at any given place. It also implies mobility, freedom of movement, and patience. Whence the decisive importance to the insurgents of the complicity of the people, a rugged terrain, and dense vegetation. Third, never engage all of one's strength in a single battle. Fourth, break off the combat as soon as it appears that losses are excessive. General Giap ordered a retreat as soon as the losses reached 50 per cent of the combatants, no matter what the situation was on the battlefield.

These maxims hold true for the defenders whatever the level of forces involved. In the adaptation of available forces and armament to the terrain and in response to the conventional superiority of the counter-insurgents, the defending insurgent has at his disposal a whole gamut of operations from isolated acts of terrorism, through guerrilla warfare, to mo-

[7] Clausewitz, *op. cit.*, p. 128.

bile warfare using a regular army.[8] One is vanquished only when one recognizes his own defeat; a single active will is all that is needed for the war to continue.

On the whole, the systematic implementation of these rules for the strategic defense compensates for the insurgents' inferiority of means and numbers. Besides, since bravery, skill, and enthusiasm make up for any lack of the characteristic military qualities of a professional army, and since the insurgents know why they are fighting and dying, the insurrection benefits from a decisive superiority in the conduct of the defense.[9] All this is in addition to the insurgents' political advantages. Does this mean they can hope for the same superiority in the attack?

The strategy of the attack, or the attempt to win. The strategy of the attack is to take the offensive with the aim of destroying the expeditionary forces of the colonial authorities. To gain victory several conditions must be satisfied. First, it is necessary to assemble insurgent guerrilla forces and to incorporate them into a regular army for the final mobile war phase. Second, massive outside help in the form of heavy and light weapons must be assured. Third, sanctuaries (mountains, forests) which offer protection from attack, especially from air power, are necessary. Fourth, one must have immediate superior strength to engage in pitched battles, although miscalculation can bring catastrophe. For example, Giap committed a serious error in judgment, which he recognized, by going on the offensive in Tonkin. The battles of Vinh Yen (January 13-17, 1951), of Dong Trieu (March 23-28, 1951), and of Day (May 29-July 18, 1951) resulted in such great slaughters within the ranks, that the outcome of the war was put off for several years. For their part, the French disdain of the fighting qualities of the fellahs and the Viet Minh was widespread and led to tragic miscalculations, especially in Indochina. Fifth, the colonial authorities may accept combat for stakes of "double or nothing" in a single battle, but it is unreasonable to assume that the colonialists will stake the outcome of the entire war on a single battle. (The counter-insurgent forces must, from the moment they have lost the initiative, assume in their turn the defensive strategy and avoid decisive combat.) Finally, it is necessary to insure that, if the incumbent has engaged in a

[8] In Indochina there were two kinds of war which were radically different: in Cochinchina there were terrorist acts and surprise attacks (guerrilla warfare in the strictest sense of the word); in Tonkin, Giap maneuvered regular army divisions. On the other hand, in Algeria, where the disproportion of forces was incomparably greater, only the first type of war was put into effect by the insurgents.

[9] This Clausewitzian truth was completely ignored by the French command.

"double or nothing" battle and lost, he should not have the will to send another strengthened expeditionary corps. The outcome of the revolutionary war hinges on an imponderable factor—national pride. (Some hegemonial powers have never experienced defeat, and do not realize that defeat is a relative thing.)

It follows from all the above conditions that a decisive victory in a single classical battle is highly improbable (Dien Bien Phu not being a model but an aberration). This is explained by the fact that the counter-insurgent's center of gravity is not the expeditionary corps but the will of the mother country to continue fighting. The logic of the conflict does not lead the insurgents to destroy the enemy's army, but to convince the politicians that the cost exceeds the stakes. This is difficult when the only stake in the war is prestige, for the defeated counter-insurgent has to find the means to disengage from a futile war without further tarnishing his prestige.

III. *The Established Authorities: Political Goals*

The political objective. In Indochina, France was willing initially to grant broad autonomy within the framework of the French Union, and planned to grant independence later—provided it would not benefit a communist regime. In Algeria there was a much greater diversity of objectives. For example, the slogan *Algérie Française* had at least two entirely different meanings: for some it meant a return to the status quo ante and the maintenance of colonial privileges; for others it meant that the Moslems were Frenchmen—equals—possessing indefeasible rights.

In general, when the colonial status quo is challenged, there are three possible responses: either one merely desires military victory followed by a return to the status quo ante or else a military victory followed by reforms designed to prevent another upheaval. The third answer would be to seek a stalemate by asking for a cease-fire. This would be followed by elections and negotiations in order to bring out the various points of view and to reach a compromise. This was the official position of the French government in Algeria from 1956 on. These three alternatives are inevitable, whoever the antagonists might be. If an authoritarian political system were to engage in counter-revolutionary war, one of the above alternatives would be chosen and imposed as the political objective. In contrast, under a pluralistic system, where, by definition, freedom of opinion, expression, and organization is guaranteed, each of these alternatives would be adopted by political parties or pressure groups. The divergences among these contradictory alternatives become all the more accentuated as the moral authority of the government becomes weak or collapses. Indeed, the executors of the pluralistic government's policy are able to implement their own political strategy in the field instead of the one chosen by the government. In Indochina several policies were used by different factions, especially by the military. In Algeria political incoherence reached such a high level that the Fourth Republic finally collapsed in May of 1958. Thus, the diversity of political objectives which is unavoidable in pluralistic governments will be all the more apparent in actual practice as the strategy of the regime falters and the government itself loses authority.

The military consequences of this chaotic political situation are very serious, for it produces incoherence in the military strategy. If the objective is the maintenance of colonial sovereignty or military victory pure and simple, then all means are justified and the colonial authorities will blindly massacre and thereby alienate the population. If the objective is the establishment of relationships of trust and equality with the population, repression will be carried out on a selective basis and will respect the rights of men and the laws of war. Consequently, repression will be weak and will encourage the insurrection. The situation becomes inextricable if these two strategies are applied simultaneously by divergent elements of the established authorities. Thus, political incoherence and contradictions have profound repercussions on military operations and lead necessarily to confusion and catastrophe in the field or to upheaval in the *métropole* in an effort to impose one and only one policy on the conduct of the war.

This confused situation has grave consequences for the counter-insurgent combatants. In fact, it becomes difficult or impossible for a soldier to know why he fights or why he risks his life. Without profound motivation, a country has only spiritless and passive troops, and therefore, an ineffective instrument. Those who are drafted probably oppose the war. Lacking enthusiasm and the proper training for this type of war, a conscript army will be mediocre. Sending professionals, who have a stronger taste for war and military glory, limits the size of the army and risks seeing it cut off from the country, and this may embitter the troops who find themselves abandoned. Public opinion, which is directly influenced by the risks run by its sons, will probably be profoundly divided. In short, counter-revolutionary war brings about a political polarization in the mother country; this can be very dangerous, weakening the regime and challenging its legitimacy.

Finally, political uncertainty has repercussions upon the rationalizations used to justify the war. Three of these have been used. First, the war could be interpreted as a fight to uphold the integrity of the French Empire. In fact this argument has been little used, undoubtedly because most Frenchmen have always been indifferent toward their colonies. There was, therefore, no hope of convincing the French people that it was urgent to make sacrifices or to die for an imperial cause. A second rationalization represented the objective of the war as the desire to spare the indigenous population a socio-political regime judged unbearable. In other words, it was necessary to convince the French that their sacrifice would save the Indochinese or the Algerians from Communism. At the very best, this rationalization is insufficient. The third justification for the war has been called the "domino theory." It affirms that if France surrenders one colony, then it must surrender all the others. This statement is certainly true, but it brings us back to the first point: there was no hope of arousing the majority of the French people by using such a threat. If by the domino theory, however, one means that defeat in one place will bring about a series of communist regimes in the entire area under consideration, many sound objections arise. The first one is that the intensification of the war is, itself, the surest guarantee of victory for the insurgent extremists. It is the cure which kills the patient. In the second place, the domino theory cannot be proven; there is no evidence that a communist regime in Algeria would lead *ipso facto* to communist regimes in Tunis and Rabat; political conditions vary so much from country to country that the domino theory has no predictive value. In the third place, even assuming the validity of the domino theory, then the question is: what happens afterwards? The final result can only be interpreted as a catastrophe if one postulates the monolithic unity of the communist bloc. One can just as well accept the opposite postulate, that the more political units there are in a bloc, the more its internal tensions compromise its cohesion and create polycentrism. In a pluralist regime, these rationalizations ineluctably reinforce division in public opinion and in the ruling elite, further compromising the unity of the policy being followed and bringing indecision into the conduct of military operations.

On the whole, these rationalizations can rally only impassioned minorities; those still nostalgically longing for imperial grandeur and those longing for counter-revolutionary crusades. Imperialists have no chance of predominating because of the complex international situation resulting from the two world wars. The counter-revolutionaries could gain the ascendancy, however, provided the crusade could be undertaken by the whole western camp. This would presuppose a movement toward political unity, a conviction of the deadly character of the threat posed by the communist bloc, and the exalted monopoly of Truth and Good. France was indeed far from fulfilling these conditions.

The problem of the colonial population. The attitudes toward the colonial population are necessarily as diverse and contradictory as the political goals of the counter-insurgents. Three basic modes of behavior accompany these attitudes. First, a realistic and logical attitude deems that the entire population is composed of actual or virtual enemies. Consequently, all military operations would be carried out without consideration for the civilian losses of the adversary; only military victory would count. Such a ruthless solution poses certain difficult technical and diplomatic problems. Futhermore, it is incompatible with the social, political, and ethical values of a pluralistic country. It is inconceivable that a democratic system nurtured through centuries, should have recourse to mass terrorism. It would be necessary first for democracy to have died and given way to a totalitarian system.

Second, an unrealistic and illogical attitude tries to make a clear distinction between national war and social war. The underlying arguments for this strange attitude can be summarized in the following fashion. The retrieval of national identity is only an ideological pretense for the insurgents which conceals real claims; these are of a socio-economic nature. Consequently, it is enough to grant agrarian reforms, to launch a bold program of economic development, and to insure the process of democratization by suppressing the old elite classes and creating new ones. This new elite class will presumably emerge from a democratic system of education open to all. Thus, the people and the majority of the insurgents will quit fighting and docilely return to the bosom of the mother country. A variation, which should take its place in the museum of ideological drollery, states that the substance of the insurgents' demands is purely imaginary and is the result of an exogenous indoctrination. An intensive counter-propaganda campaign will suffice to win over the population and thereby put an end to the insurgency. This strategy resulted in the "psychological action" in Algeria, which was based on the hypothesis that one could convince anyone of everything. It is not certain that such stupidity belongs only to France. This argument, which is so widespread in France and elsewhere, seems so strange because it does not take into account the importance of strong national passions; it assumes that man lives by bread alone. It also assumes that an aspiring people seeking redress of longstanding grievances will have more confidence in foreigners than in its own sons. All these opinions are based on such primitive psychology that they would not deserve mention if they were not so widespread.

Finally, there is the pragmatic attitude which recognizes that colonialism is anachronistic, and that its costs outweigh its benefits. The solution is to support a moderate political faction in the colony in order to undermine the extremist insurgents. This was the most widespread attitude within the expeditionary forces, at least in Algeria. Soldiers of all ranks had only mixed feelings toward the French settlers in Algeria and tended to recognize the legitimacy of the economic and social demands of the Moslems. Let us also remember that the Constantine speech of General de Gaulle, in which he announced huge investments to be poured into the Algerian economy, corresponds to the argument just outlined. This solution is possible so long as there is no war and national passions are not exacerbated. Once war breaks out the decolonization solution becomes less and less possible as the war goes on. Indeed, those indigenous leaders who support this non-revolutionary solution are recruited from the social strata which have the most to lose from the revolution, since the national revolution is gradually transformed into a social revolution. They are the propertied classes, the traditional elite, and the corrupt native bureaucracy which thrives on the economic opportunities available during a state of war. On the whole, revolutionary war produces a result diametrically opposite to the desired one: the war definitely isolates the puppet political faction from the people; it furnishes the insurgents with wonderful arguments for their propaganda and thereby accelerates the momentum of the social revolution. Thus, the established authorities find themselves cornered in an untenable position, which is the result of the contradiction inherent in seeking forcibly to convince a people to choose freely a non-communist regime.

The international milieu. What is to the international advantage of the insurrection is to the international disadvantage of the colonial authorities. France, not being a hegemonial power and finding herself in a system of alliances, was forced to rely upon her allies for matériel and political support. Even supposing that she had the means and the will, France could not have pursued a war of extermination without encountering overwhelming international opposition; this would have forced reconsideration. Furthermore, the consensus of international feeling favors decolonization and the liberation of oppressed peoples. Thus, in Indochina and Algeria France appeared engaged in anachronistic wars. There was no chance of any country enthusiastically supporting her. In Indochina, probably because of the Korean War, France was successful in convincing the American government that she was fighting for freedom. Whence came a huge amount of American aid in the form of money and matériel. However, this aid resulted in dubious relations. It was improbable that the United States, financing the French, would indefinitely allow France to wage the war as it saw fit.

General de Gaulle's accession to power introduced a new factor. He visualized France at the head of a coalition of countries which would not accept the Soviet-American duopoly, but the continuation of the Algerian war was a nullifying obstacle which had to be removed before France could again venture into the delights of great power politics. It took him four years to convince others that the war could not be won. It was to his credit that he successfully transformed a defeat into victory.

IV. *The Established Authorities: The Military Strategy*

The enemy's center of gravity. From what has been said about revolutionary warfare, it is clear that the insurgents' center of gravity is not the insurgent army (regular or guerrilla) but the entire indigenous population. This has at least two very important consequences. Even if repression is effective enough to eliminate the armed insurgents and even if few people are won over to the revolution, the insurrection will always be able to reconstitute its strength and be capable of acts of terrorism and guerrilla surprise attacks. Thus, there is no hope that repression might lead to a permanently imposed peace. It is also obvious that a classical military "vision" of the revolutionary war—i.e., the conviction that the enemy will be defeated by the strategy and tactics learned in the Conventional School of War drawn from European experiences—leads to catastrophe.

As the established authorities must soon realize, the people constitute the center of gravity, and they must direct their efforts toward the winning of the population. Four basic strategies are possible and have been used in succession or simultaneously. The first can be called the winning of the hearts. By introducing or promising radical reforms (accompanied by propagandistic Psychological Action) the counter-insurgents try to win the population over to their side. As pointed out, such a policy is of rather dubious efficacy. Besides, it has the disadvantage of accentuating tensions within the counter-insurgent camp, because some segments refuse categorically to consider reforms.[10]

[10] In Algeria the important colonists and after them the "small whites" were violently opposed to reform of any kind, since they believed that to yield on one point

A second strategy consists of the large-scale mobilization of the population by the counter-insurgents and of the systematic elimination, not only of the militants but of all groups which might be capable of being insurgent cadres. In short, it is a strategy designed to atomize the population, making it incapable of opposition. This implies an enormous conscription of troops from the mother country and the use of terrorist methods in the field. In order to hold down the number of troops required and to provide an easier and less bloody surveillance, it is necessary to displace the population to "centers of regroupment" or "shelters." In this way one hopes to isolate the insurrection from its breeding ground, the people. If such an evacuation is effected, one can be sure that it will completely fail to attain its goal. Indeed, the suffering connected with these deportations serves as excellent propaganda material for the insurgents. Because it is impossible to prevent contact between the centers and the outside, they become an excellent culture medium for the recruitment of revolutionaries. Certainly, the consciences of those in the mother country will revolt against what would look like an embarrassing reappearance of concentration camps. This policy was followed in Algeria, without much success in the field, but with violent opposition in France.

A third strategy involves the systematic utilization of cleavages which divide the population. Thus, in Indochina, a traditional enmity exists between the ethnic Vietnamese (Annamites) and the Montagnards (the Moi, Muong, Thai tribes etc.). The French mobilized, armed, and organized the latter in an effort to use them against the insurgents. They also used the religious minorities: the Catholics, Cao Dai, and Hoa Hao. But, it is impossible for the established authorities to use residual or marginal groups to build a new order that can be imposed on the majority, or to divide and rule. In Algeria tribal conflicts were used in the same manner, but with the same limitations. For example, in the Aures region an age-old hatred separated the Ouled Abdi from the Touabas. The latter having participated in the insurrection on November 1, 1954, the former *ipso facto* fell in with forces of the established authorities.

There remains a final strategy, which is simply to annihilate the population. Aside from the moral and political problems involved, this strategy meets with technical obstacles which a country such as France would find difficult to overcome. In sum, since the center of gravity is the population

would eventually mean giving in on everything. They succeeded in aborting all inclinations to reform. One interpretation of this currently heard circulating in France says that it is this obstinacy which led them to the catastrophical re-embarkment of 1962. A more conciliatory attitude would have led to the same result, but without war and its atrocities—and by means of an orderly withdrawal.

itself, the logical alternatives which the counter-insurgent is forced to face is eventual surrender or genocide. This logic determines the conduct of the operations.

The strategy of attack, or the attempt to win. If we start with the hypothesis that there is no alternative to victory, four types of war are possible. The first is *the classical war of movement* inspired by World War II. According to the best tradition, one sets up huge mechanized operations with infantry, armor, artillery, and aircraft with the intent of dealing a mortal blow to the adversary. If this strategy is used by the counter-insurgents in a revolutionary war, their defeat is assured and constant. Indeed, on the strength of the logic of the defense, the adversary will usually refuse to fight and will disappear into the countryside and into the population. On the whole it will be like beating the air. An operation of this type launched in the Aures region in 1955 did not encounter a single one of the enemy. Since "mistakes" are inevitable, to the detriment of the civilian population, atrocities resulting from conventional firepower and tactics are good propaganda for the insurgents and are an excellent source of recruitment.

Next comes *the war of territorial security* (*quadrillage*), which involves systematic occupation of the country with garrisons in each populated area. These outposts are linked to larger installations capable of sending reinforcements and tanks and of providing artillery support. Each post guards a limited sector and hunts down the insurgents. Such a strategy meets with insurmountable difficulties. The requirement for large numbers of troops would necessitate massive mobilization in the mother country—and political difficulties would inevitably arise. In addition, it is physically impossible to interdict all of the natural sanctuaries where the insurgents find refuge. The insurgent, because of his mobility, is able to concentrate relatively invincible forces against this or that outpost, destroy it, and set up ambushes against the reinforcements sent in by the "supporting" outpost. The nibbling and the loss of matériel finally exhaust the occupation troops.[11] Therefore, unless millions of troops are used, this strategy does not lead to victory.

At first glance, *counter-guerrilla war* bears the closest resemblance to the correct solution. It is based on a simple truth, which finally becomes evident to a few: the only way to win is to learn from the insurgent and

[11] Thousands of soldiers disappeared in this manner in Cochinchina. Lucien Bodard, among others, has told of the atrocious character of this war. It was guerrilla war in the strictest sense which even claimed Roland as its victim at Roncevaux.

to practice the same kind of tactics he does. The insurgent bases his strength on small but extremely mobile groups, which are almost self-sufficient and always on the lookout for an ambush or surprise attack. All that is necessary, therefore, is to form small, but highly trained units made up of volunteers and professionals, who have a perfect knowledge of the terrain and who are ready to lead a life of sacrifice and danger for weeks and months. By the systematic use of intelligence, obtained by the usual methods (torture, owing to the lack of cooperation by the population), and constant mobility, these counter-guerrilla units will give chase in order to surprise and destroy the insurgent. Tested locally and rather spontaneously in Indochina and more systematically in Algeria, this strategy has proven to be remarkably effective. .

However, the counter-guerrilla war has its limitations. The main one is the number and quality of troops required. In a far-away war with dubious or incoherent political goals, one can hope to find men qualified for this type of war only among those who have fighting in their blood and who enjoy it without worrying about the moral or political justifications for their actions. Such men can be found in every country, but they are an infinitesimal minority. Therefore, the effectiveness of an army of commandos will be inversely proportional to the extent and intensity of the insurrection. In contrast, nationalist and revolutionary passion multiplies the number of insurgent guerrillas greatly. Counter-guerrilla warfare can thus be effective and lead to victory only as long as the insurrection remains localized. Using this method, however, the British succeeded in eliminating the Malaysian guerrillas, and this method can be particularly effective in big cities. On the condition that the population of the *métropole* does not object to the means employed, such as the systematic use of torture (the *style-para*), the forces of the established authorities can in principle hold the cities indefinitely. The Battle of Algiers (1957) is a perfect example of this. In six months the paratroopers completely cleaned out the Casbah.

One must also keep in mind a second limitation. Counter-guerrilla war employs means that inevitably infringe upon human rights and the laws of war. Domestic and foreign consciences cannot help but be moved by such a war and an international campaign will be launched in order to denounce it. In a pluralist regime this campaign has an irresistably logical appeal, for it is based upon an irrefutable argument: why continue a struggle which can no longer be associated with democratic and humanitarian ideals, but which moves the nation to horror and perhaps to authoritarianism? What is the meaning of victory if its price is the loss of the national soul? A fatal split can result between the army—for whom victory is now an end in itself and not a means to a political end—and the nation which recoils at the means used for such a victory. This formula can help to define an absurd war, a war which has become insane because it has broken loose from the control of political objectives. A counter-revolutionary war, because of its inherent logic, at any moment runs the risk of turning into madness.

A third limitation is set by the outside bases of the insurrection. A counter-guerrilla war cannot stop at the borders. Should it cross them, it lends to the struggle an international dimension which might escape the control of the political leaders and arouse reactions which will destroy national and international stability. Finally, there is a limitation within the army itself. Traditional military leaders do not like restless and rebellious soldiers, either conscripts or commandos. They feel them slipping out from under their supervision and distrust their subversive potential. This distrust is transformed into hatred of political men, whom they regard as having played the sorcerer's apprentice by meddling in military affairs.

A final possible strategy is the *war of annihilation*. By the massive use of firepower, one aims to break not the will but the living forces of the adversary: war turns into a wholesale massacre. This poses technical problems. The record proves that the classical means (bombs and shells) are ineffectual over wide areas with effective, camouflaged defense. After the experiences of World War II, one is surprised that there should still exist military men and politicians who think that massive bombing could bring the adversary to his knees. Constant experience and simple psychology would indicate the certain result to be a strengthening of the will to resist and to fight. The colonial power is inevitably led to consider more radical means: the systematic destruction of crops and irrigation systems in order to starve the population.[12] If this is insufficient—for outside help can compensate for the destruction—one goes a step further into the horrors of war and uses atomic or bacteriological weapons. When it was becoming apparent that the battle of Dien Bien Phu was turning into a disaster, certain French leaders were hoping that the United States would consent to make use of atomic weapons to reverse the situation. It goes without saying that such a strategy would arouse reactions—such as intervention by a

[12] In a country which is, primarily, agricultural, the destruction of the industrial infrastructure cannot have decisive consequences; all the less since there is a defense: the dispersion into small production units. As for the complete destruction of the lines of communication, it is simply impossible.

third power—which would make its application unthinkable. International indignation would be so great that the colonial power would have to capitulate quickly or risk being discredited forever in the eyes of the world. Finally, the inevitable internal unrest would bring the regime to a state of paralysis and dissolution. On the whole, it was absolutely impossible for France to resort to such extremes. On the other hand, a hegemonial power with a totalitarian regime might not hesitate to do so.

The strategy of the defense, or the prevention of defeat. Having been persuaded of the fact that they cannot win without killing everyone, the established authorities can completely reverse their policy and decide not to lose, i.e., to hold on indefinitely in the hope that weariness will finally rally large numbers of the population to a moderate solution. But protracted revolutionary war can only benefit the insurgents. Despite its futility, the first rule that governs the counter-insurgent's defensive strategy is to avoid at any cost a "double or nothing" battle such as Dien Bien Phu, and to refuse all engagements in which absolute superiority is not certain. Second, the counter-insurgent must hold the big cities (by exercising police control), and the main lines of communication, and establish impregnable bases in strategic areas. Third, an effective and sustained counter-guerrilla war must be conducted in order to wear down the insurgents and prevent them from organizing. Finally, the counter-insurgent must launch massive and unexpected strikes to prevent the insurgent from concentrating his forces and consolidating his hold on the countryside. There is no need to add that in this case the established authorities must forego the idea of winning the hearts of the people. It is clear that such a strategy allows the war to continue indefinitely in stalemate, for insurrection has no chance of prevailing from a military point of view. It can only win politically as the war is transformed into a political struggle in the mother country; the war will continue as long as there exists the will to fight. However, a war of attrition cannot last indefinitely in the pluralistic mother country. Aside from the weariness and the burdensome costs which arise from a war whose end is not in sight, those who oppose the war can have a decisive political argument when they claim that the war has entered the absurd phase: it has become its own end, and the military objective has replaced the political goal. It is unthinkable, in a pluralist regime, that those in power will indefinitely continue their course into the absurd: sooner or later common sense will prevail.

Conclusion

The principal lesson of this analysis—aside from the fact that the organic relationship between politics and war is never so clear as in revolutionary war—can be summarized with one simple formula: all the insurrection needs is not to lose militarily in order eventually to win politically. Because of the strategic defensive advantages of the insurgents, the established authorities cannot win a counter-revolutionary war; they can only lose the war or pervert their political ideals. It would have been wiser never to have become involved in a struggle which was futile and unjustified.[13]

But if in spite of everything, revolutionary war breaks out, and its suppression is attempted, what can be done? The problem of disengagement reveals, at least as much as the military operations, the diabolical nature of revolutionary wars. How can defeat be transformed into victory? The answer to this question depends on the art of politics, not on the science of the analyst.

[13] The situation just outlined is the situation reached in the Algerian War. At no time was the French army on the verge of defeat. But, on the other hand, it could not win. At that stage, the resolution of the conflict required a political decision, and this was effected in the *Accords d'Evian.*

WALTER GOLDSTEIN

The American Political System and the Next Vietnam

A curious belief has begun to gain currency in American political folklore: that there will be "no more Vietnams." The curious factor is the verb. It asserts that another Vietnam-style war will not occur; it does *not* imply that the United States will refrain from intervening if a "limited war" should happen to break out. The distinction is critical. It is based upon the notion that three vital "lessons" were learned during fifteen years or more of costly warfare in Vietnam:

(a) That the U.S. must remain free in the 1970's to intervene in insurgency conflicts in the developing world; since the strategy of global withdrawal has been rejected, the "Nixon doctrine" advocated in Guam in 1969 must be invoked to help our friends and allies police and stabilize the developing nations of our choice.

(b) That a greater reliance must be placed upon the internal constraints of the U.S. policy process; this will arrest any repetition of the perverse escalation engineered by the Executive and approved by the Congress and the electorate during the Vietnam war.

(c) That a radical revision of the procedures of deliberating U.S. foreign policy is therefore unwise and unnecessary; the game plans for U.S. police operations overseas have been firmly corrected and there is no need to tinker with either the philosophical values

Walter Goldstein is a professor of political science at the State University of New York at Albany. Formerly a consultant to the Department of Defense, he was a visiting professor at the School of International Affairs at Columbia University between 1966 and 1970. He is now in Europe directing a research project for the Twentieth Century Fund.

or the interventionist strategies adopted by our national security managers.

The object of this essay is to question the validity of these "lessons" and to argue that a contrary belief is more supportable: *that the refusal to change the basic structures and procedures of the American political system will lead almost inevitably to another Vietnam-style war.* The pessimism of this restatement provokes no cause for political celebration. It will simply be argued that the logic of our political system is locked into the truth that Santayana stated—those who cannot learn from past mistakes are condemned to repeat them.[1]

The fascinating point about the disaster in Vietnam is that no one can explain why it occurred. That the war has failed to gain the objectives staked out by its supporters is now taken for granted. That the U. S. should never have involved itself in such a hopeless quagmire is also widely agreed. Despite the vast disillusion with the war, however, there has been no convincing explanation of why we went in so deeply, stayed so long, and failed to pull out before it escalated beyond control. Three specific explanations have been advanced, but each is too self-serving to the arguments of its proponents to be treated seriously. The career liberals insist that the Vietnam war reflects the unchecked power and the policy dominance of the Pentagon. The iconoclast liberals view it as the product of an incompetent but wilful President and of a warped bureaucratic process. The radicals of the left (or the right) argue that the military-industrial complex exercised too much (or too little) power over the customary controls of the political system.[2] None of these explanations successfully account for the enormity of a war which at a conservative estimate cost $100 billion, 49,000 U.S. combat fatalities, the uprooting of three million

[1] For an earlier analysis of the impact of the Vietnam war, written prior to the Cambodian invasion and the vituperative election campaign of 1970, see Walter Goldstein, "The Lessons of the Vietnam War," *Bulletin of the Atomic Scientists*, Vol. 26, No. 2 (February, 1970), and "Skepticism on Capitol Hill," *Virginia Quarterly Review*, Vol. 46, No. 3 (Summer, 1970).

[2] For representative arguments of each of these three positions, see Arthur Schlesinger, Jr., *A Thousand Days* (Boston: Houghton Mifflin, 1965); John Kenneth Galbraith, *How to Control the Military* (New York: Signet, 1969); and Seymour Melman, *Pentagon Capitalism* (New York: McGraw-Hill, 1970). The first accuses the professional military of systematically surrounding a liberal President with bad advice; the second assaults the top echelon of the Executive as if it operated independently of mass political support; and the last denounces the military-industrial lobby as a conspiracy of apparently unlimited power and influence. See also Melvin Laird, *A House Divided: America's Strategy Gap* (Chicago: H. Regnery Co., 1962). The company journals of the weapons industry, by contrast, depict the brilliant (though abstract) victories which could be attained through America's military supremacy if only the faint-hearted liberals in high places were vigorously disregarded.

or more Vietnamese people, and the profound alienation of a generation of American youth.

The possibility must, therefore, be considered that something is fundamentally wrong in the American political system if a wrong war can be waged for so many years in so desperate a manner. It simply will not do to blame the generals or the military-industrial complex alone; like the bureaucrats in the highest offices of the State, they depend upon widespread political and Congressional support if their hard-line advocacy is to be effective. Nor can one argue that malfunction in the mechanisms of government—or in the egregious megalomania of the Chief Executive—can account for the disaster in Vietnam. If it is to be properly understood, the war must be regarded as more than a temporary aberration of government policy or a tragic miscalculation on the part of honorable men. It was systematically conceived, justified, and executed by a civilian and military elite which summoned its best efforts to plan the bombing of North Vietnam and the forced pacification of the South. The leading advocates of the war respected the patriotic and anti-communist beliefs of the American electorate; given their sober and God-fearing demeanor, no one has charged them with committing "war crimes" in devastating so many young lives and hopeful ideals. Nor was the war in Vietnam unpopular while the illusions of a sweeping victory still survived. The war had been planned by the liberal advisers to liberal Presidents, welcomed by the conservatives in Congress, fought by the loyalist military, and supported by a counter-revolutionary nation in the name of liberal internationalism.[3] It will be argued that the power coalition still prevails today and could mobilize itself again for action tomorrow.

Most of the critiques of the Vietnam war written by academics or by former bureaucrats concur that two salient beliefs led us toward the war. First, an unsilent majority among the American people held that the forces of Communism were to be feared at all times, that they were to be contained throughout the world at nearly any cost, that they were likely to infiltrate revolutionary movements or wars of national liberation for their own evil ends, and that the United States would have to act as a coun-

[3] Robert Shaplen has written both sympathetically about the purposes of the war and critically about its execution. His latest book, *Time Out of Hand* (New York: Harper and Row, 1970), examines the global responsibilities and the tactical responses of a liberal super-power. He accepts neither the Praetorian Guard theory of why the Vietnam war persisted nor the corresponding belief that our foreign policy is engineered by conspiracy. His *cri de coeur* is that of the classic liberal who holds himself responsible for guiding the behavior of other nations but who shrinks from the pain that is caused when these nations are forced to be "free."

ter-revolutionary power, if necessary, in order to stabilize the process of international change. Acheson, Dulles, Kennedy and Johnson accepted the fact that a heavy cost in psychic and material outlays must be borne if the U.S. were to succeed in conserving a fragile status quo. As they saw it, they shouldered an obligation of grave and historical import: like Metternich they had to alert their less prescient colleagues to the threats and intrigues of the subversive regimes which surrounded them. A second sentiment prevailing in the Cold War years was also decisive in shaping the Vietnam commitment. In this belief it was held that America's purposes in world affairs were neither colonialist nor reactionary, but liberal; that its strategic planners (except in the lamentable lapse of "McCarthywasm") were oracles of liberal internationalism; and that they would put their wealthy banking and industrial interests firmly aside when they devoted themselves—as impartial servants of the State—to the definition and direction of the nation's statecraft. These two sentiments taken together can begin to explain the cultural significance of war in mid-century America and the particular phenomena of the Vietnam war.[4] The prestige leadership in both political parties utilized both of these beliefs for their own purposes. They relied upon the fear of Communism and the mystique of a strong, executive form of government to sustain the high costs entailed in liberal America's policing of the "Free World." Without facing effective opposition at home, they built the great war machine of the Cold War State to combat the evils of a supposed communist peril overseas.

To this day it is not popularly recognized that the specter of a centralized communist threat was falsely conjured up in Vietnam. In dealing with the Vietnamese insurgency against the oppressive Saigon *junta*, which had been installed and financed by the U.S. embassy, it appears that the national security managers in Washington had fallen victim to their own vivid beliefs. In their haste to defend our clients, the Saigon generals, against a popular and anti-colonial uprising, they created between 1954 and 1964 a situation ripe for revolutionary activity. Unfortunately, only their judgments were available to help define the politically feasible outcomes to be sought in the civil war in Vietnam. This ab-

[4] A theological expression of these two sentiments or pious doctrines is voiced in entertaining excess in the books published by many of the general officers who once sat with the Joint Chiefs of Staff (e.g., Taylor, Power, White, Radford, Burke, and LeMay). The deity's own expression appears in Dean Acheson, *Present at the Creation* (New York: Norton, 1969). The contrary opinion, that "great nations [tend] to equate power with virtue and major responsibilities with a universal mission," is argued by Senator Fulbright in *The Arrogance of Power* (New York: Random House, 1966), p. 9.

surd limitation of power produced the *Catch 22* style of executive war management that came to distinguish the Vietnam campaign. The managers had written their solemn books on the communist menace; they had built (after the Korean War) a splendid military machine ready for instant use; and it was their skilled intelligence which perceived (as Vice-President Johnson reminded his chief) that if Ngo Dinh Diem were "the Winston Churchill of Southeast Asia," his regime alone could suppress the threat of revolution. Since the managers listened to no one outside their inner sanctum, the self-fulfilling assumptions in their strategic designs were able to survive for several years with all their error intact. As a result, six years after the U.S. had begun to pulverize the countryside of North and South Vietnam with an unprecedented megatonnage of bombs and napalm, the management still refused to discuss their unshaken strategic belief: that in a war of national liberation, revolutionary forces can be bombed into a state of collapse and docile submission. This pious but untenable belief will probably prolong our war of attrition in Indochina long into the 1970's.

I. *U.S. Foreign Policy Options in the 1970's*

It now appears reasonable to presume that several acute tests of our Cold War axioms will be made during the 1970's. Beyond Vietnam and Cambodia it is likely that the U.S. will intervene in at least one national liberation war or counter-insurgency campaign to shore up our global alliance system. The intervention, when it comes, will surely appear in those parts of the world in which we have *either* invested significant military aid *or* deployed major strategic bases. The belief that there will be "no more Vietnams" will surely be tested in Thailand and possibly in the Philippines or Greece.[5] The *junta* in each of these nations depends upon U.S. aid to defend its weak power base against mounting forms of indigenous protest. Each nation provides air bases that are vital to the U.S. strategy of containing Chinese or Soviet expansion; and each is ruled by a *junta* as rigid and oppressive as the regime of Ngo Dinh Diem. If nationalist forces should intensify their civil war against these regimes, it is highly prob-

[5] Insurgency conditions appear most ripe in these three client states. Though none of them enjoy the close proximity to outside sources of supply which the NLF found in North Vietnam, a sufficient quantity of arms could be captured by or sold to the insurgents to wage war against unpopular loyalist forces. Revolutionary warfare could also develop in other insecure and elite-ruled societies such as Laos, Cambodia, South Korea, Malaysia, and in various regimes in southern Africa or Latin America or the Middle East.

able that U.S. military aid deliveries will be vastly increased.[6] It will then be seen whether our national security management can refuse to mount the escalating process that leads from a low level of involvement (with Special Forces, military advisers, and AID security teams) toward full-scale warfare.

The "Nixon doctrine" pledges the U.S. to assist its military allies in securing law and order from afar. But the fact remains that each of these allies relies upon defense forces that are as visibly incompetent in suppressing revolutionary fervor as the ARVN. We now cherish the illusion that our "Vietnamization" campaign has succeeded in transforming a mercenary *levée* into a national defense army. But it has yet to be proven that pacification, Winning Hearts and Minds (WHAM), or counterinsurgency campaigns can succeed even when a strong U.S. combat force enters action.[7] Self-defense forces in Vietnam, Cambodia, Thailand, the Philippines, and Greece are heavily armed with American tanks, helicopters, and small arms support; they are trained by U.S. advisers, financed by U.S. subsidies, and dependent upon an American "presence." If indigenous or insurgent units should initiate a rising against the wealthy, Western-oriented elites in each capital city, the U.S. advisers will be sorely tempted to invoke the SEATO or NATO treaties which pledge the U.S. to support a threatened ally.[8] Each nation occupies a key position

[6] Thailand has received more than $2 billion worth of aid and 47,000 U.S. troops are stationed there. They will be drawn into open (rather than covert) action if the non-communist regimes in South Vietnam, Cambodia, Laos or Thailand should fall once the main U.S. garrison in Southeast Asia is withdrawn. It is for this reason that Mr. Nixon has refused to pledge that *all* combat and air support forces will be withdrawn even after a peace settlement has been signed.

[7] A provocative essay on the stimulus to and techniques of U.S. involvement in the developing world appears in Richard J. Barnet, *Intervention and Revolution* (Cleveland: World Publishing Co., 1968). He argues that the U.S. "has seized upon the moral ambiguity of revolution to justify a global campaign to contain it, channel it into acceptable paths, or to crush it." (p. 8) An interesting modification was supplied by C. L. Sulzberger in *The New York Times*, November 15, 1970. If the United States cannot deal with insurgency situations by calling upon the techniques of "limited war," he urged that we consider the use in future conflicts of "truly tactical atomic weapons." After ten years of experimenting with chemical and biological warfare, and after defoliating millions of acres of arable land or jungle in Vietnam, this proposition is surely logical. If it were ever implemented, our "body count" teams could declare any civilians vaporized by our nuclear fall-out were *ipso facto* enemy units driven underground by our successful bombardment.

[8] Of the $25 billion in military and other aid supplied by the U.S. (to countries outside Europe, India, and Laos) between 1946 and 1967, $22.6 billion went to such military allies as Iran, Korea, Pakistan, Taiwan, Turkey, Thailand, and Vietnam. (See the testimony of AID in the *Special Report* given to the House Foreign Affairs Committee in 1967.) The aid given to Laos, at about $200 million each year, was the highest per capita received by any nation in the world. The total aid figures admitted in public are often misleading as many "surplus" weapons transfers were

in the regional alliance structure which supposedly contains communist expansion. Judging from past experience and present rhetoric any insurgency movement will likely be viewed as composed of subversive agents or "outside infiltrators" working in the interests of Peking, Hanoi, or Moscow.

The scenarios for American military suppression in Phnom Penh or for "Philippinization" in Manila have surely been programmed in the Pentagon by the veterans of Hamburger Hill, Khe Sanh, and My Lai. The principal task of the military, after all, is to prepare contingency plans and worst-case estimates for all future crises. It is now known that plans for our massive bombardment of North Vietnam were laid out long before the dubious naval incidents in the Tonkin Gulf provided the opportunity to initiate an undeclared war.[9] It has also been admitted that ten years of clandestine operations in Laos paved the way for Mr. Nixon's decision to rush U.S. troops to the defense of the Lon Nol regime in Cambodia.[10] It can be safely concluded, therefore, that the Joint Chiefs would be found derelict in their duties if they failed to prepare contingency plans to rescue each of the vulnerable allies which we have subsidized for over twenty years.

II. *The Politics of the Cold War State*

Several political factors must be weighed in considering these gloomy projections of future war. First and most important, the deployment knowledge and the computerized intelligence data of the CIA, the National Security Agency, and the Joint Chiefs provide the civilian security manage-

---

made in secret specifically to avoid Congressional scrutiny. This point was illustrated by Senator Fulbright in the 1970 hearings of the Joint Economic Committee when the Comptroller General and other financial officers were unable to confirm whether U.S. military aid overseas was now running at the annual total of $5, 7, or 8 billion.

[9] A fascinating analysis of the combat which did *not* take place in the Tonkin Gulf and of the contingency plans to rush ahead with the bombing of North Vietnam can be found in Joseph C. Goulden, *Truth is the First Casualty: The Gulf of Tonkin Affair—Illusion and Reality* (New York: Rand McNally, 1969). Tom Wicker, in *JFK and LBJ: The Influence of Personality Upon Politics* (New York: Morrow, 1968) adds one unconfirmed detail (pp. 224-225): The timing of the Tonkin Gulf Resolution was perfect for LBJ's 1964 election campaign. "... a few weeks later, a White House official in a position to know confided to me that the President had been carrying around the text of the resolution 'in his pocket' long before the Tonkin episode gave him the right opportunity to lay it before Congress."

[10] An informed estimate holds that anywhere from 17,000 to 27,000 air strikes *each month* have been made against Laos since 1968, turning large areas of the countryside into devastated "free-fire zones." Congressional approval for a war in Laos has, of course, never been solicited. See *The Indochina Story* issued by the Committee of Concerned Asian Scholars (New York: Bantam, 1970), pp. 45-48.

ment with sufficient leverage to dislodge many of the traditional constraints implied in the Constitution. It is no longer necessary for a military *coup d'état* to seize the offices of the State, in the style of *Seven Days in May*, if another undeclared war is to be initiated. The able civilian elite who serve as the President's court of advisers can operate sufficiently well in an emergency to rush troops into action and to serve the Congress with an irreversible *fait accompli*. Several troop formations are always ready to move, executive agreements with allies were secretly concluded long ago, and a public formula to justify pre-emptive action can be speedily prepared. The national security managers have had twenty years of training to define the "national interest" and the "feasible" parameters of strategic planning in their own hard-line terms. Their authority in the past has been immune from political criticism and their institutional influence has been embellished with bipartisan prestige and mass media adulation. The Joint Chiefs can be counted upon to provide almost automatic support for their rapid military decisions while the "opposition" critics can be safely disregarded. The critics do not know their way through the White House corridors of power or the Capitol cloakrooms where senior Senators exchange "Eyes Only" information morsels. Nor do the critics recognize when they have stumbled upon the extravagant claims that have been advanced to conceal intelligence failures or to placate interservice rivalries.[11] The managers are unusually adept at operating in large organizations (like the giant automobile corporations or the Wall Street banks) and they know how to keep privileged information from unfriendly critics and from the untutored public. Indeed their personal fascination with the arcane powers of the State is so compelling that they naturally feel contempt for the "Nervous Nellies" who question both their policy judgment and their political authority.

As a second political factor, the master planners in the Pentagon and

[11] General Westmoreland and Ambassador Bunker gave the most glowing reports to the Congress about the exhaustion of NLF forces and the success of the pacification programs just prior to the 1968 Tet Offensive. Mr. Rostow, on the White House staff, and Ambassador Komer in Saigon cited the computerized print-out of the Hamlet Evaluation System to argue that 67 per cent of the South Vietnamese population lived in secure areas. Each of their claims was exploded by the offensive. Critics and Congressmen shut off from the President did not know that the size of the adversaries' forces (and their casualties) had been monstrously exaggerated and that many of the "secure areas" were thoroughly penetrated by the NLF. The "daisy chain" of misinformation is described in Townsend Hoopes, *The Limits of Intervention* (New York: McKay, 1969), but even his account fails to reflect the magnitude of an intelligence failure which could systematically collate false reports in 40 of the 44 provinces of South Vietnam—and then program an annual war effort costing $30 billion on the strength of the warped judgment of the Embassy in Saigon.

in the White House basement have shown themselves to be remarkably skilful in avoiding the democratic requirements of public disclosure and critical debate. They know what executive agreements have been made, what weaponry has been transferred, and what forces have been deployed among the more insecure nations of our global alliance system. Though the Congress is supposed to authorize these arrangements and the mass media to publicize them, the national security elite has been free to negotiate secret arrangements with Spain, Thailand, or Greece to supply their officer corps with U.S. weapons or to pledge support to their counter-insurgency activities. In several remarkable cases the Senate Foreign Relations Committee declared it knew nothing about these commitments, while the State Department could not even produce the appropriate documents for the Committee's review.[12] Senator Symington (a former Secretary of the Air Force) tried hard to surface the executive agreements that had been negotiated with our client prince in Laos, but the Senator has yet to divulge any information that his subcommittee succeeded in eliciting from the managers' closed files.

It is unwarranted, therefore, to ascribe the root causes of our Vietnam fiasco to the professional military and to their powerful allies in Congress and in the defense industries' lobby. The civilian leaders of the war establishment have been more energetic and influential in determining the military content of our foreign policy than the generals or their industrial friends. Several studies have shown that this new civilian establishment has been recruited from a small group of high status professionals, most of whom have spent the last twenty years at the apex of our institutional hierarchies.[13] This mandarin group of a few hundred men includes the

[12] A list of the military actions initiated without Congressional authorization can be found in *Global Defense: U.S. Military Commitments Abroad* (Washington: Congressional Quarterly, Inc., 1969). Both the Senate and the House committees on foreign affairs published surveys (in 1970) of the formal treaties and the informal agreements that had led to U.S. deployments overseas; but the surveys contain no hard definitions of the circumstances in which local U.S. forces could be used in Spain or Thailand to combat internal uprisings against our military allies. It was for these reasons that the Senate adopted a "national commitments" resolution in 1969, and the Fulbright, Cooper, Church, Hart and Hatfield amendments to military authorization bills in the subsequent year. In most cases, however, these resolutions cannot prevent the Commander-in-Chief from deploying or activating U.S. forces in troubled areas; they simply ask that the Senate be consulted and advised ahead of time. At the present time, the intent of these legislative gestures has been totally disregarded—except in those few cases in which a token compliance required no sacrifice of the Executive's authority.

[13] Greater sophistication has been brought to the study of policy elites since C. Wright Mills wrote his pioneering work, *The Power Elite* (New York: Oxford, 1956). For example, Gabriel Kolko, in *The Roots of American Foreign Policy* (Boston: Beacon, 1969) uses careful data to show that the social origins of the leading

prominent Washington attorneys, the Ivy League professors, the Wall Street bankers, and the foundation directors who have occupied practically every one of the key political positions in the CIA, State, Defense, and the National Security Council since 1948. As the guiding force of the policy establishment (no matter which party holds the White House), the managers have devoted themselves to the Higher Cause of arming America—both for its own good and for their own advancement.[14] Ironically, while General MacArthur warned President Kennedy against committing U.S. troops to fight in the jungle wars of Asia and General Eisenhower struggled to curb the inflationary expansion of the defense budget, the academic systems analysts and the Harvard Law School graduates of the New Frontier were bursting with enthusiasm to redefine our nuclear deterrence posture, to establish paramilitary combat units, to swell the overseas role of the armed services, and to prove (as in Vietnam) that military technology can triumph in any situation of revolutionary warfare. It is vital to note that the decision to wind down the Vietnam war was taken only after these liberal enthusiasts had grown tired of their fascination with military force.[15]

policy makers are less important than the values they hold in common. They might not look or act like an elite, in the classic sense, but they act predictably toward enhancing the material gain and the political status of the powerful. It is difficult to prove the fact of elite manipulation in a mass society; but it is more difficult to prove that "those with power" have been ready either to resign on principle or to penalize their own self-interests. See also William C. Domhoff, *Who Rules America* (Englewood Cliffs, N.J.: Prentice Hall, 1967) and David Horowitz, editor, *Corporations and the Cold War* (New York: Monthly Review Press, 1969).

[14] Kolko, *op. cit.*, pp. 12-29, and Richard Barnet, *The Economy of Death* (New York: Atheneum, 1969) provide detailed sociological studies of the few hundred men who have moved back and forth between the top echelon directorships of the public and private institutions of power since the Cold War began. While avoiding a vulgar Marxism in their analyses, they show conclusively that both the fortune and the prestige of this establishment has been built upon a high level of military preparation. It is instructive to list the number of occasions on which senior officers—who now head large corporations or banks—were asked to consult with the White House as new diplomatic crises broke. Generals Taylor, Clay, and Norstad, along with a host of former Secretaries of Defense or State, have often attended the emergency planning sessions of subsequent administrations. Indeed, the shuttling of prominent bankers between Wall Street and 1600 Pennsylvania Avenue is reported to have stilled many of the Soviets' worst fears during the 1962 Cuban crisis!

[15] On March 25 and 26, 1968, the Senior Advisory Group on Vietnam met in the White House to discuss whether the war should be further intensified—as the Joint Chiefs had urged—or whether the "winding down" should commence. The notables present were influential not only because of their former management of public power but because they spoke with the authority of the Wall Street boardrooms or the Washington law partnerships which *every single one* represented. The Senior Group, according to Hoopes (*op. cit.*, pp. 214-215), included three famous generals, Acheson, Ball, Bundy, Dillon, Vance, Dean, Murphy, Lodge, and McCloy. All were prominent captains of industry or international bankers who had retained their

Arthur Schlesinger, Jr. has noted that our postwar "warrior caste" has been moved by the Stimsonian belief "that an orderly world requires a single durable structure of world security . . .;" the credo insists that "if aggression were permitted to go unpunished in one place, this by infection would lead to a general destruction of the system of world order."[16] This vital dogma is the source of the "liberal evangelism" that has accelerated the momentum of the military machine and encouraged the definition of diplomatic goals in the language of security threats. It has helped promote the excessive militarization of our statecraft and our paranoid view of political change among developing nations. Moreover, the sophisticated use of the language of threat has impressed the "attentive publics" who follow the "cues" of the powerful and the prestigious.[17] Universities, church and civic groups, and Councils on World Affairs invited the more eminent of the managers—whose distinction in business and in government had been *equally* celebrated in the popular press—to assure their audiences that military technology coupled with moral vigor (and a higher defense budget) would prolong the American century of world peace.

The limitations of this commanding group were revealed in a striking manner in Vietnam. For all the strenuous intelligence services which they commanded and the miraculous "captured documents" which they cited (but rarely revealed), the national security managers were unable to define who were the enemy and what were the political objectives of the war. This failure of political imagination proved to be of decisive significance. The managers refused to believe until 1968 that the NLF was an indige-

---

high level contacts in government. When they complained (as did McGeorge Bundy of the Ford Foundation) about the soaring economic costs of the war, they were seriously regarded because of their impressive commercial status, on one side, and because of their military habit of ignoring moral or theoretical questions, on the other. No "dove" clergymen or academic critics achieved a comparable policy influence, no matter how clear-sighted their policy views might have been.

[16] Richard M. Pfeffer, editor, *No More Vietnams?* (New York: Harper and Row, 1968), pp. 7-10. It is striking that among the numerous contributors to this volume, those least critical of the war were the first to argue that *no* lessons should be drawn from Vietnam (pp. 2-4)—and that there will be "No More Vietnams" (p. 39).

[17] The tendency of "attentive publics" to follow the policy "cues" of prestige power-holders and opinion-leaders is explored in Gabriel A. Almond, *The American People and Foreign Policy* (New York: Harcourt, Brace, 1950). A pungent satire on the policy elite and its deferential audiences appears in John Kenneth Galbraith's novel, *The Triumph* (Boston: Houghton Mifflin, 1968). His wry description of the industrialists who attend the "off the record" sessions at the Council on Foreign Relations' sanctum on Park Avenue is painfully accurate. Throughout the Vietnam war the periphery of the policy establishment found valuable support in the conservative journals and academic institutes which specialized, along with the executive managers of industry, in promulgating hard-line definitions of diplomatic "realism."

nous and popular entity. Nor could they define which political forces could succeed in winning national esteem in Saigon. For four years they refused to admit that the saturation bombing of South Vietnam would smash into pieces the "nation building exercise" in which we were supposedly engaged. The obduracy of the managers in this regard was matched only by their political myopia. While Professor Rostow in the White House basement called up B-52 assaults on the DMZ, it came as a surprise to McGeorge Bundy that the aerial bombardment of Hanoi would do more damage to the structure of American society than to North Vietnam.[18] Dean Rusk's attitude toward peace proposals reflected his experience in another wealthy foundation: no proposal could be considered if its supporters attacked the status of the awarding committee. Secretary McNamara's application of systems analysis to the pacification of a peasant people will probably become known as the Edsel symbol of absurd political engineering. It may be surpassed in time, though, by the expectation of Professor Kissinger that the entire adversary command network (COSVN) would dally in Cambodia while we visibly completed our preparations for Operation Total Victory (sic). The thought was apparently lost to him, as it was to his predecessors, that it is easy to sweep into a country like Cambodia but virtually impossible to find a sufficient alibi to sweep out again.

The accidental accumulation of poor intelligence, the faulty leadership in the Congress and in the White House, and the disregarding of political criticism cannot explain how so many errors could be compounded by four successive Administrations. Obviously, little credibility should be left in the argument that the political system worked well—despite the errors which it sustained—and that radical revisions are therefore unnecessary. Unfortunately, all too much faith in the virtues of the present system still survives.[19] It is highly logical to suppose that this blindness of faith will

[18] A careful analysis of the war has been written by a former top bureaucrat, Chester Cooper, *The Lost Crusade: America in Vietnam* (New York: Dodd, Mead, 1970). He found that (p. 432) "Senior military officers, Walt Rostow, Secretary Rusk, and General Taylor . . . have a bombing hang-up." Of course, bombing a peasant regime to the bargaining tables was seen as neither immoral nor ineffective. "I had a heated argument with Walt Rostow one afternoon about a scheduled raid on targets close to the Hanoi airport," he adds. "I lost. The bombs fell." Mr. Cooper's refusal to protest on principle was shared by every liberal critic in the Johnson Administration.

[19] Typical of the faith invested by "value free" political scientists in the virtues of the system is the conclusion of Laurence I. Radway in *Foreign Policy and National Defense* (Atlanta: Scott, Foresman, 1969): "In the last analysis . . . the United States stands to gain from the exceptional learning capacity of its political system. The belief that it will, in the end, follow the path of restrained liberalism stems from a sense that American democracy . . . possesses to an exceptional degree the ability to detect and correct its own errors. This is the positive virtue of a civil society in which power is widely shared . . ." (p. 182).

lead us into disaster when an opportunity to enter the next Vietnam presents itself. If we continue to believe that the consensus attributes of the system will constrain our national security managers and that the rhetoric of checks and balances will preserve a constitutional form of foreign policy, the rush into the next revolutionary confrontation will be virtually inevitable. Piety alone has never stopped a determined group whose resort to power, however impious in character, has been justified with strong theological authority. It can be argued, of course, that the mood of the electorate might change its theological beliefs about anti-communist interventions and that another Eugene McCarthy could emerge in the 1972 primaries to dislodge the present war President. But it should be recalled that the popular uprising of 1968 only produced pro-war candidates in both parties and that this experience could be repeated again in a time of national stress. Furthermore, the electoral defeat of the outspoken "peace" candidates in 1970 suggests that the political party system still balks at criticisms of the fundamental defects of our system and its policy values.

III. *What Ever Happened to the Countervailing Powers?*

Three modes of argument have been used to explain why the political system produced such poor policy choices during the Vietnam years. The first and most pragmatic relies upon a critique of our political institutions. This mode has produced marginal criticisms of recent Presidential leadership, of the superior efficiency of the Pentagon compared to that of the State Department, and of the inability of the Congress to exercise its watchdog scrutiny over public policy.[20] But it has failed to explain why no serious effort was made to correct the thorough and continuous misuse of power. In short, there is faith rather than conviction in the arguments of the critics of institutional power. They assert that the next Vietnam will not occur because instrumental adjustments and self-correcting mechanisms can be fashioned from the experience gained in the Vietnam war.[21] But the record of recent experience weighs heavily against their belief.

The second mode of argument is exclusively ideological in character.

[20] A sampling of these criticisms can be found in: Tom Wicker, *op. cit.;* Adam Yarmolinsky, "Bureaucratic Structures and Political Outcomes," *Journal of International Affairs*, Vol. 23, No. 2, 1969; and Stanley Hoffmann, *Gulliver's Troubles* (New York: McGraw-Hill, 1968), part III.

[21] Cooper concludes (*op. cit.*, p. 462): "...the lesson has been driven home: the United States is not likely to go to war again without a clear mandate from Congress, and the role of the Congress in major questions of war or peace cannot be budged, hedged or dissembled." It would appear that Mr. Cooper believes that a declaration of war has recently been voted or that our intensive combat involvements in Cambodia and Laos are fictions invented by the mass media. No effort by the Con-

On the right, there are conspiracy insinuations that Mr. McNamara suppressed the Joint Chiefs' plans to annihilate Hanoi or that President Johnson was intimidated by the anarchic (and communist-financed) protest movements on the campus and thus lost the nerve to atomize our Asian adversaries. On the left the critics argue that imperialist expansion and aggressive war-making are necessary to the survival of a corrupt capitalism dependent upon defense profits. In the middle of the spectrum, unfortunately, the ideology of the silent majority and middle America is no less intransigent—and no less despairing. The arguments here congeal around the consensus doctrines of *raison d'état:* the President must be supported in times of war, moral doubts about our devastation of Vietnam must be suppressed in the national interest, and political debate must not only cease at the water's edge, but a bipartisan commitment to our struggles overseas must be maintained at all costs. It appears that the very vehemence of these "moderate" arguments will prompt us to repeat our intervention against communist or nationalist insurgencies in the next few years.[22]

The third mode of argument is the one that is least pursued. It is of greatest concern to the present analysis. There used to be an axiom of democratic politics that countervailing powers must be brought to bear in the execution of a nation's statecraft. This was to be accomplished by institutionalizing the checks and balances of constitutional government and by encouraging minority opinion in searching political debate. The terror of the Vietnam years has shown that neither institutional checks nor the political expression of dissent could thwart the momentum toward disaster. The Congress failed to inhibit the waging of an undeclared war; the Executive failed to curb the headlong process of escalation; the political parties failed to mobilize opinion against a profitless bloodletting; and the mass media (together with other informal agencies such as the universities and the churches) failed to reflect the profound distress and frustra-

---

gress to inquire into U.S. combat fatalities or aircraft losses in these wars has elicited the admission of Executive accountability which the Constitution requires.

[22] It is tempting to cite the rhetoric of Mr. Nixon and Mr. Agnew on America's democratic duty to protect the freedom of our military allies in Asia, but it is more to the point to quote from Roger Hilsman, *To Move a Nation* (New York: Doubleday, 1967). As a former Assistant Secretary in the State Department, he nimbly reflected the "liberal" dynamics of the policy system: "McNamara, [General] Taylor, and the Joint Chiefs of Staff were not so convinced" that the war "was fundamentally political. They were less worried about the consequences . . . of the repression" imposed by Diem and Nhu; "they were more sympathetic to the argument that Vietnam really needed a certain amount of authoritarianism if it was to beat the Viet Cong." After all, they, themselves, "had made so many public statements that we were winning" (p. 496).

tion which settled on the American people. The grave significance of these failures can best be appreciated by summarizing briefly why each of the countervailing powers was unable to arrest the mad momentum of a hopeless war.

1. *Executive complicity*. Though every Administration seeks to unify the diverse policy interests and the bureaucratic thrusts of the separate departments, it is expected that adversary debate and intramural conflict will preserve a "relative openness" (as Hilsman put it) in the policy councils of government. Specifically, top echelon officers in the State Department are expected to draw upon their classified information and upon CIA briefings to prevent the Defense Department from foreclosing the President's options. Refugees from the Johnson Administration have revealed that intramural conflict ceased soon after the Dallas assassination. As a result, CINCPAC felt free to issue the incredible victory predictions uttered by General Westmoreland; and the President's own adviser, Professor W. W. Rostow, went unchecked on television with dubious reports about the successes won in the pacification of the Vietnamese people.[23] Only after the Tet Offensive had wiped away the cosmetic of "public relations warfare" was the truth revealed that the CIA had disagreed with all of the factual estimates—of enemy body counts and liberated hamlets—which the Joint Chiefs had confidently publicized.[24]

Most doubters in high places had evidently been silenced by the time that the clandestine war in Laos and Thailand had moved into higher gear. The fiasco of the Bay of Pigs invasion had been repeated a dozen

[23] The best illustration of truth-burying in the Executive appears in Hilsman (*op. cit.*, p. 510). A deal was struck in 1963 that "McNamara and the Joint Chiefs would agree to a policy of 'pressure and persuasion' on the Diem regime, which they now thought was unnecessary [to Hilsman's horror] ... but they would agree only if the White House and the State Department would in turn agree to a public announcement that the Pentagon was right about how [well] the 'shooting war' had been going." A remarkably similar trade-off between the news releases of the political and military lieutenants in Hitler's GHQ was negotiated after the collapse at Stalingrad in 1943.

[24] A high American pacification official held that "Another place where clear-and-hold has been proceeding remarkably well is in Quang Ngai. I think that Quang Ngai is going to turn out to be one of the success stories of 1967." The next year Quang Ngai province was the scene of the My Lai incident. Quoted in Jonathan Schell, *The Military Half* (New York: Vintage, 1968), p. 212. Another optimistic prediction of victory: "Tactical airpower, U.S. Air Force style, had its first chance to prove itself in a guerrilla war ... in South Vietnam. The results were extremely impressive. So impressive, in fact, that not even the most ardent airpower advocate could fully appreciate the degree of success unless he had been in the right spots in Vietnam and had actually witnessed the results." Cited in Colonel James A. Donovan, USMC (ret.), *Militarism, USA* (New York: Chas. Scribner's Son, 1970), p. 104, from *Air Force Magazine* (March 1966). Schell's book describes in horrifying detail these impressive results of airpower.

times as the Pentagon East announced its Pyrrhic victories at Khe Sanh, Hue, Ia Drang, and My Tho. As the former Commandant of the Marine Corps revealed, while the military services competed for larger deployments and larger victory claims, no one with authority stopped to ask what had actually been won and at what cost.[25] When the military machine finally ground into reverse (in March 1968), it was seen that their estimates were thoroughly spurious and that a cabal of Senior Advisers would have to intercede with the President if the Joint Chiefs' commitment to disaster were ever to be halted.

2. *The Congress.* The Legislature is supposed not only to encourage adversary debate and information disclosure within the Executive, but also to exercise an independent scrutiny of the Administration's strategic designs. It is difficult to defend its performance on either score. The most powerful committees of the Congress—particularly, Appropriations and Armed Services—refused to question the data and the war plans of the military. Indeed, they more often shielded the Joint Chiefs from the prying doubts of those few "doves" on the Hill (such as Morse, Gruening, McGovern, Fulbright and the House liberals) who exposed the frequent inconsistencies in the Pentagon's testimony.[26] Six years too late the Senate came to repudiate the Tonkin Gulf resolution, which the Johnson Administration regarded, incredibly, as "the functional equivalent" of a declaration of war against North Vietnam.[27] The damaging course of escala-

[25] General Shoup USMC (ret.) issued a fiery denunciation of inter-service rivalry and collusion as a means of misleading public opinion in "Our New American Militarism," *Atlantic Monthly* (April, 1969). His theme is explored in greater depth in Colonel Donovan, *op. cit.* Both authors illustrate how the military bury unfavorable reports in order to enhance the prestige and the status of the budget requests advanced by each of the armed services.

[26] Considerable surprise was expressed when the Senate's conservative Appropriations Committee at long last turned skeptical of the ABM procurement requests, the glowing Vietnam reports, and the urgent entreaties for larger budgets which the services brought before it year after year. In 1970 it not only cut the $71 billion defense appropriation bill by 3 per cent but it also attached a rider to the bill prohibiting the use of the funds to "introduce U.S. ground troops into Laos, Thailand and Cambodia." (*The New York Times*, December 4, 1970). This reiterated the text of the Cooper-Church amendment to the Senate's foreign military sales bill which the House, characteristically, refused to accept. The Administration encouraged the conservatives who dominated the Senate-House conference on the appropriation bill to demand a "loophole giving the President wide discretionary authority" (*The New York Times*, December 30, 1970). In the end the conservatives conceded some sacrifices in rhetoric to the Senate "doves," but they retained the President's right to finance any actions of the South Vietnamese and "other free world forces" needed to support the Government of Cambodia or Laos. In concrete terms, this legislative confrontation revealed how little the Congress had learned about the possible abuses of the war powers by the largest military establishment yet known.

[27] A compelling account of why the Senate allowed itself to be led into voting such an open-ended Resolution appears in Tom Wicker, *op. cit.*, pp. 221-226. It had

tion and poor policy planning went unchecked from 1954 to 1967; it was not until the first major disaster occurred, in the Tet Offensive of 1968, that the Congress dared to intervene. Defense budgets approaching $80 billion had been approved in the later years only after the most cursory of debates. No dissenter from within the Administration was pressured to reveal the cost overruns that distorted each of the major budget procurements or to divulge his informed doubts about the strategic rationale of the war. In 1966, Mr. McNamara calmly admitted to an underestimate of $10 billion in his accounting on Vietnam while the cost of the 300 to 400 planes lost over North Vietnam has never been finally settled. As a result of its own lax and acquiescent performance, the Congress failed to engage in that demystification of public policy which the Legislature alone can perform in a highly bureaucratized society.

The Congress defaulted in its watchdog and inhibitory duties for two basic reasons—neither of which have been removed. First, the antidemocratic rules of Congress, which are built largely upon rural overrepresentation and the seniority system, encouraged the more aged and conservative of the Congressional leaders to shield the military from critical exposure or public debate. Representing secure and usually Southern districts (many of which housed large military installations), the leaders were too often concerned about the renewal of local defense contracts to worry about "unpatriotic" and minority criticisms of the military's wisdom.[28] Committee chairmen like Stennis, Russell, Rivers, Mills, and Speaker McCormack surely saw enough classified documents to question the accuracy of CINCPAC's reports or the Joint Chief's procurement requests. As far as the Congressional Record shows, however, they frequently utilized their formidable powers to shut off debate or to quash demands for investigative hearings and rarely permitted an open vote on motions critical of the Administration's policy. In the House, indeed, it was easier to mobilize enthusiasm for rhetorical or patrioteer resolutions than to question inflationary authorizations or to review the

---

not occurred to Senator Fulbright, the floor manager of the Resolution, that the Administration would use its ambiguous language in order to legitimate an open-ended commitment to the war.

[28] As Secretary of Defense, Mr. Laird has run into stiff questioning only from the Foreign Relations Committee of the Senate. He briefed it and the Armed Services Committee on a recent U.S. assault on a POW camp in North Vietnam. But he could not understand why the former, alone, was outraged by his failure to disclose that bombing strikes had been resumed close to Hanoi at the same time. He answered those questions which were asked, he noted, but it was not his responsibility to tell the Committee which questions to ask (*The New York Times*, December 1, 1970). The Congressional leadership failed to comment on this astonishing interpretation of Executive responsibility.

vicious use (as in Project Phoenix) of U.S.-subsidized pacification programs.[29] The senile leaders in the House controlled the behavior of unreliable and doubting juniors, who came largely from industrial and two-party districts; this left few opportunities for the majority to challenge the entrenched leadership of a small but dominant cabal. That the cabal has survived, with a few slight changes in membership, through three Administrations is reason enough to redefine the term "contempt of Congress."

A second cause of Congressional failure can be seen in its refusal to fulfill the roles of educating public opinion and exercising its "magisterial" arbitration over public policy. Testimony was developed by Fulbright, Symington, Proxmire, and others to demonstrate that the Administration's explanations of the Tonkin Gulf incident, the clandestine war in Laos, and the financial costing of the war in Vietnam were shot through with distortions and inconsistencies. All too easily, unfortunately, their testimony could be ridiculed by the President, deluged with counter-publicity by the Pentagon's 400 full-time lobbyists on Capitol Hill, or condemned to obscurity by the mass media.[30] In the end, the refusal of the President to consult with the Congress (or with the State Department, it appeared) in planning the invasion of Cambodia was historically well justified. The Congress had resigned itself long before to a passive role in adjudicating matters of war and peace. It had exerted itself to intervene actively on budget allocations and contract procurements, but it ignored the larger strategic issues of nuclear deterrence or revolutionary war. Both chambers had helped keep alive the Cold War enthusiasms urged upon them by the national security managers, and few of its members found it exorbitant to spend 70 per cent of the public revenues on the sustenance of a vast military machine. Once the Congress abandoned its constitutional role of raising an army or declaring war, it seemed all too willing to share with the security management its last great power, over the purse. It helps in no way, therefore, to lament the Executive's usurping of the war powers when the Congress has demonstrated time and again that it is unable and unwilling to share in their control.

[29] The blemished record of the Congress is reviewed in great detail in Barnet, *op. cit.* The ruthlessness of committee chairmen in curtailing debate on the military budget or on atrocity accusations in South Vietnam is to be compared only to their clamor to resume the bombing of North Vietnam.

[30] Successive Presidents and their advisers were able to exploit the bipartisan leaders on the Hill by drawing them into their counsel. "If he is skillful and ruthless enough, a President can use [this device] as a means to reduce Congress' capacity to act meaningfully on foreign policy issues." Dorothy B. James, *The Contemporary Presidency* (New York: Pegasus, 1969), p. 144. This was demonstrated vividly in the bipartisan amity of Johnson and Dirksen or between Nixon and Speaker McCormack during six years of religious war-making.

3. *Mass communications.* The centralized control of news exercised by the television networks and the national wire services has complimented the shift toward the centralization of public power. At least until 1968 the mass media gave highly favorable treatment to the Administration's arguments and film footage of the war. This often made the critics and dissenters appear freakish, hysterical, and defeatist. The silent majority was entertained on the dinner-hour news program with a rich variety of Presidential speechlets, with helicopter assaults on insurgent strongholds, and emotional footage of military hospitals and funerals. A few "talk" programs—lacking in vivid video images or action photography—occasionally explored the real issues of the war: the untenability of the Saigon *junta*, the ruin of Vietnam's social fabric, and the complex arguments about a possible peace settlement. But no way was found to put the arguments against Mr. Rusk's dismissal of peace overtures on the front pages of the tabloid press or to review the accuracy in the last two years of Mr. Komer's reports on the pacification program during prime time viewing hours. Indeed, a fury greeted the first reports in the quality press of the civilian destruction wreaked by our bombardment of Hanoi: their correspondents were accused of sending eyewitness reports that caused anxiety to our pilots. Mr. Agnew found his own style and mission in savagely attacking the elite directors of the mass media and the metropolitan press for questioning the sincerity and altruism of President Nixon's peace proposals. Though his assault upon the effete and impudent snobs of the campus won him a nationwide television audience, his attacks began to falter. The media had begun to discover its audience's curiosity about military mismanagement and executive deviousness. After the outcry against the Cambodia invasion, it dared for a few weeks to comment on the questionable political purposes and side effects of the war.[31] When the 1970 mid-term election opened, however, the relapse of the mass media into traditional preoccupations with the candidates' wives, tailoring, and television styles quickly replaced the criticism once aired about the conduct of the war.

The powerful role of the mass media must not be underestimated. The directors of the media argue that they are obligated to meet the profit expectations of their corporate shareholders. They are not required to conduct an academic seminar or an independent examination of the national security bureaucracy and the quixotic procedures of the Congress.

[31] An earlier attempt to assess the televised reporting of the war and of political dissent appears in the present author's "Network Television and Political Change: Two Issues in Democratic Theory," *Western Political Quarterly*, Vol. XX, No. 4 (December, 1967).

When the President pre-empts prime time and banner headlines to announce that an emergency in Cambodia requires a prompt, aggressive response, they have usually stalled for some while before questioning the wisdom of his judgment. It is only after the military emergency has subsided and the policy issue has lost its drama (as in the invasion of Santo Domingo), that the mass parts of the media will dare to be critical. In any case, public opinion tends to be slow in turning against the authority of official pronouncements. Hence, a "cultural lag" has tended to grow, separating the media consumers from the personalities on the page or the screen. The caution of the mass media executives has greatly weakened the countervailing checks against official manipulation and error which only the centralized media services (whether they like it or not) can exercise. So long as Dr. Stanton of CBS or Julian Goodman of NBC refuses to indicate doubt about the official reports and film footage which they broadcast, they can only be viewed (along with their advertisers) as propaganda agencies incapable of political neutrality. Unaccustomed to objective standards in their "public service" performance, they will become an even greater liability to society once it determines to restrict the field of public cant.

4. *Political pluralism and the political parties.* The necessary base of the Executive's war powers must be built upon an engineered consensus. Short fuse actions like the Bay of Pigs or the Santo Domingo invasions can always be launched before political forces at home are aroused, but lengthier and more costly initiatives require the nurturing of domestic support. It is on this score that the national security management has developed unprecedented skills. Its refinements in the arts of consensus engineering are based upon good psychology and the success borne of long practice. Only a small minority will be well enough informed to recognize that a President's seizure of a military initiative is *not* a unique historical event or that his political timing fits into a larger and more suspect pattern of behavior.[32] Too often majority opinion remains innocent of such Machiavellian calculations, believing cheerfully in the accurate in-

[32] The fascinating similarity between the call to arms in the Tonkin Gulf Resolution of 1964 and the unconstitutional manner in which President Polk declared war on Mexico in 1846 is explored in Samuel E. Morison, Frederick Merk, and Frank Freidel, *Dissent in Three American Wars* (Cambridge, Mass.: Harvard University Press, 1970). The violent dissent generated by the wars of 1812, 1846, and 1899 suggests that minority opinion has always been suspicious of an Executive which advertised its own "responsibility" while precipitating violent and irreversible action. Yet it is rare that the minority can prevent the slide toward war, especially if a fleeting and tyrannical majority (as Hamilton put it) should be clamoring patriotically for violence and blood.

telligence and the shrewd perception of the national security managers. Since many Congressmen find it unprofitable in their local election races to raise complex questions about national strategy—even though they suspect that another fiasco is brewing—they judge it the better part of discretion to ignore the matter or to resign themselves to the secrecy of the Executive in all complicated issues of war and peace. The blatant refusal of most Congressmen to discuss the costs and dangers of the Vietnam war provides gruesome evidence of how fear and conformity can dissolve any sense of restraint in a "representative" form of government.[33]

The record of the national parties and of local Congressional candidates on these issues can properly provide cause for alarm. In the long Vietnam years they cultivated a consensus built largely upon ignorance, fear, misplaced patriotism, and a "puzzling mixture of bellicosity and friendliness in our responses to the alien world."[34] But the lack of information and intellectual structure in a mass political culture results in acute experiences of cultural fatigue. Public opinion allows its moods to be recued or its prejudices to be reinforced—unless it has grown too weary or suspicious. Thus, rather than tangle with ancient shibboleths about honoring Cold War commitments, "out" party candidates find it easier to resort to the political style of personality contests or muted policy exchanges in their election campaigning. This evasiveness reduced the Presidential election of 1968 to a plebiscitary choice between two like-minded candidates, both of whom shared the "liberal" belief that a strong President and a concentration of power in government are vital to the discharging of ominous defense obligations.

Admittedly, changes have occurred in recent years in the thrust of political campaigning. Domestic issues have acquired a greater impact, youth has been drawn into a limited form of participation, and money

[33] The author observed several of the debates in the 1970 election campaign that were staged by two incumbent Congressmen who, due to the quixotic form of redistricting practised in the state of New York, were obliged to run against each other. The Democrat was a religious and hard-swinging "hawk," the Republican a timid and inarticulate "dove." Both avoided discussing the war as far as they could. While the Democrat praised Mr. Nixon's military wisdom, his opponent chose to speak on the pollution of the environment. Both waxed eloquent in judging students and angry dissenters as "irresponsible" members of an otherwise pacific society.

[34] V. O. Key, *Public Opinion and American Democracy* (New York: Knopf, 1961), p. 213. Key had raised the problem (p. 554) of how there can be a responsible leadership of opinion on foreign policy issues when informed debate is limited "by the necessities of external unity and by diplomatic secrecy." In asking "the influentials" to resolve the problem he failed to anticipate the credibility gap of the 1960's and the bipartisan drive to replace divisive debate with a patriotic consensus.

has begun to matter a great deal more—particularly for the purchase of television time. Though candidates have become more photogenic, they have not become more daring or knowledgeable in their handling of the substantive issues of foreign or military policy. The "dove" candidates often have to rely upon their folksy local appeal (like Fulbright in Arkansas or Gore in Tennessee) once they leave Washington; and their party usually refuses to nominate them for high office once they appear to be too deeply identified with skeptical or unpopular positions. Adlai Stevenson, John Kennedy, and Hubert Humphrey were mainstream liberals. They never associated themselves with the critical opposition in their electoral campaigning. Their friends and close advisers had served in the management of previous Administrations; invariably, they cautioned against diminishing the executive authority of the President or retreating from a hard-line position on NATO, the supposed missile "gap," or on the conduct of the Vietnam war. Since the Republicans shared these policy positions too (after Eisenhower had entered his lame duck period), and since third party candidates were barely audible—with the exception of the Wallace-LeMay team—this left the control of the nation's war powers as a nonissue in the mind of the electorate.[35]

IV. *American Politics in the 1970's*

Several pessimistic conclusions must be drawn from this analysis. First, it is likely that the United States will be provoked to remount the escalation-into-war process once again in the 1970's; an intervention in a revolutionary conflict somewhere in our alliance system can be safely predicted. Second, few of the countervailing powers which we believe to be extant will be effective enough to deflect the national security management from the pursuit of military strategems or diplomatic manipulations among our weaker friends and allies. Opportunities and inducements to intervene in Third World insurgencies will surely present themselves with great frequency. Our containment and alliance commitments will surely help justify our combat involvements in the name of preserving a stable world order and the credibility of our alliance pledges. It appears

[35] A wealth of attitudinal and polling data has been collected by skilled sociologists in Milton J. Rozenberg, Sidney Verba, and Philip E. Converse, *Vietnam and the Silent Majority* (New York: Harper and Row, 1970). They examine the Eugene McCarthy and the Kent State protest movements and explore (p. 45) "the depth of antipathy of most Americans to any political dissent that goes beyond the confines of conventional debate." In short, they find that radical protest and criticism provoke a harsh cultural response. If the strategy of the dissenters is to change policy rather than to shock the established and the comfortable, they must learn to be more devious in their appeals.

equally probable that the consensus dynamics of our political system will facilitate rather than impede a further call to arms. The Congress and the President have done nothing to reduce the authority of the national security management; nor do they even appear to be worried about the management's poor record of performance. Neither party has resolved to reverse an allocation of priorities which allots $178,000 for the killing of each (claimed) Viet Cong while paying a federal subsidy of $55 a year for the education of each American child. The Executive departments, the political parties, and the mass media have learned little from our harrowing experiences in Vietnam. Twelve thousand GI's have been killed since Mr. Nixon first hinted that he had a plan to end the war, but little evidence is visible to suggest that the managers will make the political concessions necessary to negotiate a peace settlement. The suspicion survives that they either want the Vietnam war to continue or that they still lack the political imagination needed to end it.

The fact that the political system has been unable to deal with the Executive's control of the war powers does not mean that the problem can be ignored. An overwhelming majority in the Senate endorsed a National Commitments Resolution in 1969. The Senate draft presents the character of the problem which the President and Congress recognize but refuse to resolve.

> Already possessing vast powers over our country's foreign relations, the executive by acquiring the authority to commit the country to war, now exercises something approaching absolute power over the life or death of every living American—to say nothing of millions of other people all over the world. . . . The concentration in the hands of the President of virtually unlimited authority over matters of war and peace has all but removed the limits to executive power in the most important single area of public life.[36]

The intent of this resolution was to remind the national security management that a democratic system requires that the Legislature must "warn, consult and advise" (as Walter Bagehot put it) even on matters of foreign and military policy. It is significant that the Senate played no greater role in the conduct of the war in Vietnam, Cambodia or Laos after 1969 than it did prior to the adoption of its pious rhetoric. For its part, the Administration urged, in seeking the defeat of the Cooper-Church and Hatfield Amendments to the 1970 military authorization bills, that their rhetoric be repudiated:

[36] Cited in Dorothy James, *op. cit.*, p. 138.

> It is bad policy to seek by legislative action to restrict the power of the Commander in Chief on matters which clearly come under his constitutional authority. The administration does not plan to send military advisers or combat personnel to Cambodia. However, any such operational limitations ought to be self-imposed by the executive. Congress should not attempt to force them on the President through statute. . . . Furthermore, adoption of such an amendment would no doubt have a seriously adverse psychological effect on the Government of Cambodia.[37]

It is regrettable that seventeen years after the narrow defeat of the Bricker Amendment the Senate should have to return to the issue of hobbling the Executive's power. Senator Bricker sought to inhibit the President's authority for the wrong reason; he and his allies wanted to foreclose the diplomatic choices of the Executive. President Eisenhower argued that the Congress is not the proper body to deal with matters of secrecy and dispatch in foreign policy. It is not equipped with the means of acquiring sensitive information or of deciding upon the subtle and urgent problems of international negotiation. As Mr. Eisenhower discovered, the House in particular, suffers from a serious "cultural lag" in its views of a fast changing world; it has consistently perceived communist or revolutionary forces in Southeast Asia or the Middle East through the satanic visions which John Foster Dulles bequeathed to it. Moreover, the seniority principle imbued in the committee system tends to insure that the most aged, inflexible, and secretive members will remain as the most powerful of committee chairmen. The dilemma at the core of our political system, therefore, remains unresolved. If the Legislature cannot take over the bureaucratic functions of the Executive and if it will not assert its control over the skilful managers of the national security mechanism, then what alternative resolution can be suggested?

The dilemma is more grave than any other facing the nation as it enters the 1970's. The threat posed by urban blight, racial tension, and the pollution of the nation's resources pale in comparison, perhaps because no ready solutions are at hand. The countervailing powers cannot be restored unless the procedures of government are fundamentally changed. The Congress, the political parties, the mass media, and the "attentive

[37] The text of the official memorandum submitted by the State Department to the House Foreign Affairs Committee appears in *The New York Times*, December 4, 1970. It is worth noting that the memorandum went only to the House, to bolster its opposition to the Senate's amendments, and that accidental disclosures have revealed that U.S. "military advisers and combat personnel" have indeed been active in Cambodia, Laos, and Thailand—despite the Administration's bland denials.

publics" have shown little concern with the excessive concentration of the war powers. They have been even less concerned about modifying the Cold War shibboleths which drive us toward confronting each and every national insurgency which emerges within the sacred zones of our defense alliances. The first serious rumor of revolutionary activity in Manila or Athens or in the mountains of Thailand will reawaken all of our messianic promptings. So long as the national security managers can authoritatively define the "national interest" when the discussion of the threat and a military response first emerges, they will meet no effective opposition from the embassy staffs overseas, from the power structure on Capitol Hill, or from the nonmilitary departments of the Executive. After all, who will listen seriously to the argument that the rebels in Luzon or Bangkok are more popular and worthy of our support than the political generals whom we have financed for so many years? Of course, the managers have been shrewd enough to recognize one consequence of the Vietnam war. The public's fatigue and the inflationary impact of greater defense spending require that some modification must be made in their future plans. But the important point about their adjustment maneuvers is that they need surrender no part of their political authority or of their privileged status if these marginal modifications are programmed with professional care. The continuing dominance of the managers—once the retrenchment gestures have been made (as in the 3 per cent cut of defense expenditures)—bodes ill for the nation's statecraft in the 1970's.

The ability of this establishment to either design or slide into another Vietnam is almost unlimited. Its eminent staff has learned little from the sophisticated but disastrous mistakes of the past, and it requires nothing but blind faith to believe that they will refrain from repeating past mistakes in the future.[38] As a noted political scientist wrote, in gauging the "pressure exerted" by the agencies of national security upon the representative institutions of government:

> Since World War II these bureaucracies have been in a strategic position to inflate national security needs in order to advance either their expansionist goals as organizations or the career ambitions of their

[38] Chester Cooper, *op. cit.*, pp. 460-461 concludes his bureaucratic and "value free" analysis with the astonishing prediction that Congress and the American people will be enthusiastic for no further Vietnam ventures. Nor will they "permit any President once more to lurch or slide into war by executive decree. The Tonkin Resolution will not soon be forgotten; there will be no more blank checks. . . ." One wonders if his liberal faith is shared by the civilian and military managers who are now rising to fill the top places in the national security hierarchy.

> members. "Created by wars that required it, the machine now created the wars it required."[39]

A leap of faith, rather than a reliance upon rational change, will be needed if one is to assume that the innate goodness of the electorate or the benign operation of the political system will guard us against future abuses of the war powers. But faith, like credibility, depends upon a clear recognition of the prudent behavior of the powerful. Their record to date is sufficiently discouraging to chill any such faith.[40]

In conclusion, it seems that we must now choose between consolidating the war powers of the Executive and its massive bureaucracy or strengthening the democratic controls over the machinery of the State. We cannot perpetuate the present confusion—in which institutional energies and resources are made ready for war while electoral debate and political aspirations are deceived by the expectation of peace. The critical lesson that we should have learned from the Vietnam war is that the constraints of the political system are too feeble to contain the authority of the national security management within the confines of democratic politics. We cannot rely upon technological refinements or administrative sophistication to provide a functioning compromise. The problems involved are too complex to be handled with facile optimism and a pragmatic tinkering with the mechanisms of popular government. Our basic choice lies between reordering the power structure and the political forces which nurture it; or submitting to the *raison d'état* and to the engineering of consensus which will move us toward the next war. The choice before us must be viewed in the light of our contemporary political culture. Simply affirming that there will be "no more Vietnams" will be as ineffectual as declaring a war on poverty while reserving most of the available public revenues for the self-serving weapons scares of the military and its industrial lobbies. If we are ever to reduce our anxiety and our well-fed paranoia—that as the leading superpower we must fight for every hour in the sun—it is vital that we discard the two principle

[39] Francis F. Rourke, in Robert E. Osgood *et al.*, *America and the World* (Baltimore: The Johns Hopkins Press, 1970), p. 185. The concluding quotation is taken from Joseph Schumpeter's classic work on the military bureaucracy of ancient Egypt.

[40] The largest plurality of the century was obtained by a President who campaigned in 1964 on the pledge that "We are not going north and drop bombs. . . . We don't want our American boys to do the fighting for Asian boys. We don't want to get . . . tied down in a land war in Asia." (cited in Tom Wicker, *op. cit.*, p. 231). The credibility "gap" emerging from these pledges and the later inquiry into the Tonkin Gulf Resolution impaired popular confidence in the prudence and candor of government.

axioms of our political value system: (a) that it is our messianic duty to maintain a sufficiently high level of armaments to intervene whenever and wherever our alliance commitments should require it; and (b) that the "flexible response" and "instant preparedness" doctrines of the Cold War State require a tight, secretive, and self-perpetuating control of the war powers in the offices of the national security managers. These axioms are based upon widely shared beliefs and upon a strong set of institutional arrangements within the political power structure. Until the axioms are finally challenged, and then reversed, there is every reason to suggest that the opening of the next Vietnam war will be a "natural" consequence of our present beliefs and practices.

Another way of stating our ultimate choice has been formulated by Lewis Mumford in *The Myth of the Machine: The Pentagon of Power.* We are in the grip of a Faustian confrontation between the superb technology of military weaponry and of institutional organizing, on the one side, and of "divided powers, tenacious traditions, embarrassing historic contradictions, confusions, compromises and obscurities" on the other.[41] The disaster in Vietnam has begun to undermine the popular belief that our technological ascendancy and our moral virtues—as Mr. Nixon interprets them—can serve to legitimate the reordering of an emerging world. But it has not taught us how to reorder the values of our own power structures or how to harness the energetic authority of the "permanent war" establishment. Until we learn to curb the efficient operations of this prestigious establishment, and the ideology of protracted conflict upon which it subsists, one must assume that the political system, itself, will create the next Vietnam. Its dynamic is that of war preparation and executive control and its philosophical position is that of "arm to parley"—*so long as both activities are held under firm control.* The political culture which supports this form of government is not easy to change. It has survived the monstrous shock and despair of the liberals' war in Vietnam while learning little about liberal internationalism or the liberal view of the Cold War State. Given this poor learning performance, it will be logical if the snares and delusions of the next Vietnam should spring upon us before we finally explain to ourselves what happened in the last one.

V. *Epilogue*

It is tragic that the invasion of Laos should confirm the central argument of this essay even before the printer's proofs were pulled. The extension

[41] (New York: Harcourt Brace Jovanovich, 1970), p. 180.

of the war into Laos was designed, according to Mr. Nixon's State of the World message, both to protect the withdrawal of American troops in Indochina and to accelerate the winding down of a war that has already lasted twice as long as World War II. The more durable of Mr. Nixon's critics, who failed to understand this bizarre logic, tried to remind him of the Cooper-Church Amendment, the repeal of the Tonkin Gulf Resolution, and the endorsement of the National Commitments Resolution which the Senate had passed in its attempts to restrict the Executive's unbridled usage of the war powers. The President apparently ignored the substantive as well as the constitutional objections raised by the critics; knowing the limitations of the political system, he correctly perceived that there was neither precedent nor persuasion enough to force him to change his position. The *realpolitik* of his position was revealed when a small group of Senators threatened to legislate a new prohibition upon the use of American combat forces or military aid—this time in the invasion of North Vietnam for which the Saigon *junta* now clamors. Administration spokesmen retorted, exactly as they had done two months earlier that: (1) the prerogative powers of the Commander-in-Chief could not be curbed by legislation; (2) any such Senate initiative might increase American casualties on the battlefield; and (3) no plans had been made (as was once said of Cambodia and Laos) for U.S. forces to enter action in North Vietnam. The resumed bombing of North Vietnam did not enter into the category of war actions as this was, in Secretary Laird's immortal phrase, only a "limited operation." It is little wonder that Chairman Fulbright, who has been publicly called a "security risk" and a wilful "defeatist" by top staff in the White House, should concede that the Congress can do nothing more to limit the momentum of war in Indochina.

In a recent discussion Professor Galbraith took issue with one of the arguments of this essay by contesting the emphasis placed upon the "liberal evangelism" of the national security managers during the Vietnam years. The elite directors of the war establishment were never liberals, he argued, and many of them had never even voted for the Democrats prior to 1960! The fact remains, however, that all of them were appointed to office by a liberal President and that *none* of their actions or policy advice was ever repudiated by such liberal standard-bearers as Adlai Stevenson, the Kennedy dynasty, or Hubert Humphrey. Though the Cold War credo of Acheson, Bundy, Rusk or Taylor was decisively rejected in the A.D.A. definition of American liberalism, these elite advisers agreed fully with the cardinal axiom of the Harvard-Washington liberal: a strong President must assume full command over the war powers of a nation locked into an unending struggle with the world-wide forces of revolution and Communism. Only McCarthy, at the head of his children's crusade, mocked these beliefs; and he was roundly abused by the elite liberals who hoped to take office in a Humphrey administration.

Perhaps one can distinguish, in the light of Professor Galbraith's objection, between two types of liberals—those who worry about the domestic environment and those whose beliefs go even further than the water's edge when they regard the problems of change overseas. The trouble with the latter group is that they have been eloquent in condemning the excessive influence of the Pentagon but fearful in criticizing the forced pacifying or napalming of popular insurgency movements in Southeast Asia. Another maverick out of the liberal mainstream, Senator McGovern, has dared probe into the chill silence surrounding the My Lai war crimes trial. If war crimes are defined not by attitude but by morality, he has suggested, we should worry not only about the murder of local villagers but about the aerial assault on Vietnam's cities, towns, and countryside. We must then ask CINPAC, the Joint Chiefs, and the White House who authorized the selection of targets. The mainstream liberals, unlike McCarthy and McGovern, have not only shrunk from attacking the foibles of the Washington power structure, but they have remained totally silent about all of the moral issues of the Vietnam war. Their political timidity and their meliorist faith in the system have only served to strengthen the hands of the national security managers as they continue in their necessary obligation to program the next Vietnam.

It is tragic, therefore, that the searing pain of Vietnam must be associated so directly with the confusion and doubt of contemporary liberalism. The fact remains, however, that liberals—whoever they are—tend to be concerned about, and eager in, the mobilizing of the countervailing powers in the political system. That they have so often defaulted in mobilizing the checks and balances against Executive authority in recent years can be ascribed to their personal sense of uncertainty. Faced by a hopeless war, which they have long condemned, they have shown more concern for preserving the traditional privileges of the Washington establishment than for preventing the annihilation of hapless villagers in Asian free-fire zones. So long as this uncertainty and political conventionality survive they will never succeed in playing a forceful role in checking the crusading violence of the war directorate. In the last resort, it will be because of the naive liberal belief that the political system can be representative, sophisticated, and just—even without undergoing fundamental reform—that the national security management will feel free to initiate and orchestrate the next experiment in the personal excitements and the institutional errors of mass violence.

JOHN H. HOAGLAND

Changing Patterns of Insurgency and American Response

To understand why insurgencies created such a strong set of responses in Washington during the 1950's and 1960's, we need only examine a list of local conflicts since World War II. The best available compilation lists over 50 local conflicts of a military nature in the less developed world from 1945 until the late 1960's.[1] Sixteen were interstate wars, none of which, with the single exception of Korea, provoked a direct U.S. military response, and only a few of which led to other forms of involvement. Twelve were colonial wars which uniformly prompted a "hands-off" policy, at least at the declaratory level. Most important, however, were the 25 conflicts which can be characterized as primarily internal in nature, usually involving irregular or guerrilla forces pitted against an established government and often enjoying strong outside support. Here one finds a comparatively high degree of U.S. involvement in one form or another, based on what Bloomfield and Leiss have called "the litmus-paper test" of "the fear of major Soviet or Chinese advantage."[2] This fear was usually

[1] Lincoln P. Bloomfield and Amelia C. Leiss, *Controlling Small Wars: A Strategy for the 1970's* (New York: Alfred A. Knopf, 1969), Appendix C.

[2] *Ibid.*, p. 396. Varying degrees of U.S. involvement, in the form of intervention or military training assistance, were present in at least the following insurgencies: Philip-

---

John Hoagland has been concerned with international defense and arms control problems, especially in relation to the developing world. He has served both in government and in private research organizations and is currently the head of John H. Hoagland, Inc., of Wellesley, Mass. His articles have been published widely in American and European journals including *Orbis, Europa Archiv, Schweizer Monatshefte,* and *Military Review.*

based on evidence of Soviet or Chinese support of or contact with the insurgents. The fact that Washington has occasionally, as in the Dominican episode of 1965, been guilty of an instinctive response, without adequate analysis, should not obscure the fact that a harsh conditioning process preceded the implanting of this reflex response.

Some of the main questions that now confront Washington are the following. Is insurgency in its classical sense still an important threat to the security of less developed countries? If not, what, if any, are the new or different threats? When and to what extent will threats to the security of these countries fall within the purview of U.S. policy interests? Will we be either willing or able to do much about such threats? Finally, will we be able to identify any central sources of the orchestration of violence in the Third World? As a starting point, it might be helpful to review some of the knowledge we have already acquired about insurgencies during the last 20 years. Our emphasis will be placed on the accessibility of weapons and matériel with which irregular warfare is waged, not because the material aspects are ever the most important, but because they give us a specific and comparatively simple means of probing this complicated topic.

The Mechanisms of Insurgency

In a short but useful book on guerrilla warfare, Paret and Shy have described the campaigns and writing of T. E. Lawrence, leader of the Arab revolt against the Turks, as marking "the advent of the guerrilla leader-theorist, consciously, imaginatively, and systematically employing an unorthodox military weapon."[3] In his own writing on guerrilla warfare, Lawrence described many of the features that one finds later in the writings of Mao Tse-tung and Che Guevara. One of his key points was that "irregular troops are as unable to defend a point or line as they are to attack it."[4]

Lawrence's tactics were generally based on the judgment that "perhaps the virtue of irregulars lay in depth, not face."[5] He likened the Arab guerrilla to "a thing invulnerable, intangible, without front or back, drifting about like a gas."[6] In this description Lawrence has identified both

pines, Lebanon, Cuba, Congo, Laos, Guatemala, Greece, Dominican Republic, Bay of Pigs, and of course, Vietnam.

[3] Peter Paret and John Shy, *Guerrillas in the 1960's* (New York: Frederick A. Praeger, 1962), p. 25.

[4] See Lawrence's brilliant essay on guerrilla warfare published in Vol. 10, Fourteenth Edition of the *Encyclopaedia Britannica*, p. 950.

[5] *Ibid.*

[6] *Ibid.*, p. 951.

the strength and the inherent limitations of irregular insurgent operations. They must avoid open, fixed battles, and therefore cannot, by themselves, wage decisive frontal warfare on the government's source of strength in order to break that strength and acquire power for themselves. Just as Lawrence's revolt of Arab irregulars was intended mainly to support Allenby's frontal operations, the insurgent leader normally attempts to incite or hasten a course of events that he cannot bring about by himself.[7]

The guerrilla leader must be continually aggressive in order to achieve the necessary impact on world opinion; on the other hand, he must never risk defeat.[8] Consequently, the guerrilla force usually conducts a very economically planned campaign of surprise ambushes and hit-and-run attacks against the enemy's weakest outposts, seldom achieving major military objectives. If it is operating alone, the guerrilla force must hope that its efforts to undermine the authority of the government in small ways will create an environment in which other actions can be taken. Or, more importantly, the guerrilla force can operate in conjunction with a main force of regulars, as in Vietnam and in the Arab revolt.

A second inherent limitation is the secrecy with which guerrillas must operate, a requirement which limits the scale, location, and terrain of their operations. Normally the insurgent must base his operation in difficult or remote terrain. In such areas, as Paret and Shy point out, there are seldom any profitable targets to attack. More important, the problem of obtaining arms, ammunition, food, medical supplies and other equipment is rendered even more difficult than it would be otherwise. As a result of these and other limitations, at some point the successful insurgent leader faces the decision of "going public," that is, of changing to the conventional tactics of open warfare, which require greater firepower, fixed bases (whose location will become known by the enemy), and well established external sources of supply. For all of these reasons, the guerrilla leader often decides against taking this step; or having taken it, determines to revert to guerrilla tactics, unless, as in Ho's rebellion or the Biafran secession, he is able to acquire and hold territory, people, and the related accoutrements of a legitimate government.

In the Algerian War, as in the Greek Civil War, the insurgents reached a point at which they began to stage fixed battles with regular forces, using

[7] Obviously the exceptions to this statement are important—e.g. Cuba and China; and these exceptions normally depend on abnormally weak or inept national or colonial leadership.

[8] For an excellent discussion of the limitations of guerrilla tactics, see Paret and Shy, *op. cit.*, pp. 31-36.

heavy weapons. In both cases, heavy losses were sustained, supplies were difficult to acquire, and eventually the irregulars reverted to the hit-and-run tactics of classical insurgency and later—as their fortunes continued to decline—to crime and terrorism mainly in the cities.[9] Terrorism should be recognized as the lowest point on the continuum of anti-government violence. Often it produces a dramatic effect for the effort involved, but remains relatively incapable of achieving any substantial objective unless the government is especially inept, or its major foreign allies especially nervous. The converse of this point is that once the insurgents revert to guerrilla warfare or terrorism, it is often virtually impossible—as the Vietnam experience shows—for the incumbent government to stamp out all evidence of their presence. Hundreds of thousands of U.S. troops in Vietnam cannot prevent an occasional, carefully planned "spectacular."

There is one factor which permits the flow of arms and matériel to the insurgents on a much broader scale and often leads to a situation generally approximating interstate war. This is the provision of support and sanctuary for the insurgents by a neighboring state. As Sir Robert Thompson has pointed out:

> A long jungle frontier cannot be sealed off. It is a waste of time and resources to build forts, frontier roads or forces, all of which will tie down a large body of troops for no effective purpose. Nothing can prevent small parties of men crossing such a frontier at any time.[10]

Several insurgencies of the past and present evince the importance of open borders to support the insurgent. It seems likely that future insurgencies, capable of meeting the "litmus-paper test" of "the fear of major Soviet or Chinese advantage," will likely occur mainly in regions contiguous to those states or their proxies.[11] There are several current examples in Southeast Asia, not only in the associated states of Laos, Cambodia, and Vietnam, but also in Thailand and, perhaps less obviously, in northern Burma and in the Indian states of Assam and Nagaland. The capability and willingness of Communist China to provide clandestine support and sanctuary for insurgents across national borders will remain consider-

[9] See the case study of the Greek Civil War in Lincoln Bloomfield, Amelia Leiss, *et al.*, *The Control of Local Conflict: A Design Study on Arms Control and Limited War* (Washington: USGPO, 1967); for a detailed account of the Algerian War, see Gene R. Harris' study in *The Control of Local Conflict: Case Studies*, prepared for the U.S. Arms Control and Disarmament Agency by Bolt, Beranek and Newman, Inc., August 1969 (Vol. III).

[10] Sir Robert Thompson, *Defeating Communist Insurgency* (New York: Frederick A. Praeger, 1966), p. 154.

[11] *Supra*, fn 2.

able in the 1970's. In Burma, for example, the continuing struggle of the government to control insurgency in the Shan and Kachin states—insurgencies conducted by the White Flag Communists presumably with the matériel support of China—indicates the presence of latent security problems in Southeast Asia for the U.S.

At least in their early stages, insurgencies have most often been very small in size, a characteristic dictated by the need for extreme security. Later, of course, if the insurgency is successful, the numbers may grow rapidly. In Bolivia, however, Guevara's band was probably never larger than about 50 men and women, and available evidence indicates that he badly overestimated the readiness of the country to accept a revolutionary insurgent movement, possibly on the basis of overly optimistic reports from the Bolivian Communist Party.[12] Che himself has written: "It is not always necessary to wait until all the conditions for revolution exist: the insurrectional focus can create them."[13] In practice, it seems likely that the conditions must indeed exist plentifully before an insurgency can succeed, and that the skill of the insurgent leader must be matched by government weakness and/or ineptitude.

Turning specifically to the question of weapons, small arms provide the basic firepower of the insurgent. Light, rugged weapons which can be stored in hidden caches, and which use light ammunition and require little maintenance, are his most needed arms. Insurgents usually acquire their weapons by smuggling, theft or capture, occasionally by direct receipt from a major power, or collection of remaining stockpiles in a former battle zone.[14]

Smuggling, with the help of outside sympathizers or commercial suppliers, often involves the support or acquiescence of an interested foreign government. Examples are the EOKA insurgents on Cyprus, who received arms smuggled in fishing boats from Greece; and the Algerian F.L.N., which acquired weapons from many sources through the United Arab Republic and neighboring countries. Weapons were smuggled from Egypt across Libya and through the Sahara into remote mountainous areas of

[12] See Russell J. Bowen's study of the Bolivian insurgency in *The Control of Local Conflict: Case Studies*, Vol. II, p. 27. With regard to the Bolivian insurgency, Bowen asserts that "One cannot escape the feeling that the decision of Guevara to initiate guerrilla activities in Bolivia when he did was prompted more by the pressure of events in his own life than by a truly objective consideration of the needs of the continental revolution."

[13] *Ibid.*

[14] See John H. Hoagland and Priscilla A. Clapp, "Notes on the Small Arms Traffic," Publication C/70-7, Arms Control Project, Center for International Studies, Massachusetts Institute of Technology, March 1970.

Algeria. Given the risks of running the French blockade (which was very thorough), weapons and ammunition became very expensive.[15] In fact, the effectiveness of the French blockade, by denying the Algerian insurgents all the weapons and ammunition they needed, points to the fact that while no embargo can ever be totally effective, a restriction of supplies can often be achieved where the insurgents do not enjoy a long, unpatrolled border with a sympathetic neighboring country.

Insurgent doctrine calls for the theft or capture of military small arms and ammunition from the national forces as the principal source of supply. Examples are the raids of the Cuban insurgents on the arsenals of Batista's army; seizure of government arsenals by insurgents in the Dominican crisis; capture of weapons in the field; and raids on rail or road shipments of weapons and ammunition. A common error of government forces has been inadequate protection of their own stock of military weapons. During the Cuban insurgency, Castro's forces were able, once the tide of the insurgency had turned in their favor, to capture thousands of weapons and tons of ammunition that had been supplied by the United States to Batista for counter-insurgency purposes. One striking instance was in December 1958, when Batista sent up a poorly armored train, heavily loaded with weapons, to relieve the besieged city of Santa Clara. As a result, the train itself became the prime target of the insurgents and was easily captured.[16] As Castro himself has stated: "I always believed that there are far more weapons in a barracks than you can import in tons of oil and grease and so on."[17] In the later phases of his insurgency, Castro estimated that 85 per cent of his weapons had come from captured stocks. Of course, in the beginning, the insurgents almost totally depended upon smuggled weapons and could not capture weapons until after the strength of their movement had sufficiently grown.[18] Similarly, in the Dominican crisis, the rebels were able to arm themselves almost entirely by means of raids on government arsenals and police stations.[19]

[15] See the Algerian case study in *The Control of Local Conflict: Case Studies*, Vol. III, pp. 82-83. Similarly, in the Kurdish insurgency against the national forces of Iraq, smuggling of weapons by private traders was the main source of supply. As in most similar instances, the costs rose very high. For example, a single rifle round cost the Kurds up to $1.40. (See Glenn M. Cooper's case study, Vol. III, p. 173.)

[16] See Priscilla A. Clapp's informative study of the Cuban insurgency in *The Control of Local Conflict: Case Studies*, Vol. II, p. 129.

[17] Fair Play for Cuba Committee, "Fidel Castro Speaks on Marxism-Leninism," cited in *The Control of Local Conflict: Case Studies*, Vol. II, p. 133.

[18] *Ibid.*

[19] See the Dominican case study in *The Control of Local Conflict: Case Studies*, Vol. II, p. 200. It is interesting to note in this regard the not infrequent incidence of raids on National Guard armories in the United States, such as the raid in Newbury-

Four other methods of obtaining arms have also been important to the insurgent. These are:

1. Confiscation or voluntary contribution of arms from the civilian population. In the Cypriote independence movement, for example, the EOKA confiscated hunting rifles and other personal arms from the local population.[20]
2. Direct sales or assistance from a major power. In relatively few instances, an insurgent group has enjoyed this kind of support. Examples are the U.S.-supported insurgents in Guatemala and Cuba, the Egyptian and Iraqi support of Al Fatah, and Chinese support of various African independence movements. (This does not include the more important cases already cited, such as Greece and Vietnam, where an open border permits direct support of the insurgency at a very high level of activity.)
3. Cottage manufacture of bombs and explosives from captured dynamite, etc. Such manufacture has been known to include the production of rifles.
4. Collection of weapons left in battle zones after a major conflict, or weapons left behind by a departing colonial power. The Japanese, for example, left weapons stockpiled throughout Southeast Asia that are still being used by insurgents. Similarly, the French left great quantities of weapons when they evacuated Indochina.

With regard to the last of these methods, the Huk insurgents in the Philippines were armed largely with weapons left in the area after World War II. U.S. stockpiles were sold as surplus after the war, but control over ownership was very lax. There is little doubt that tighter post-war U.S. control of its own and Japanese weapons in the Pacific would have had a suppressive effect on the Indonesian and Philippine insurgencies. Eventually Magsaysay, as part of his very effective counter-insurgency program against the Huks, began paying a bounty for weapons. From 1950 to 1955, this effort brought in 89,000 small arms.[21]

In light of the enormous quantities of small arms already in the world inventory and the very high rate of annual production, it seems doubtful

---

port, Massachusetts in September, 1970. A participant in the raid is alleged to have said, after his capture, that the armory was chosen because of its remote location and because of the likelihood that, as a Corps of Engineers' armory, it would contain explosive devices.

[20] See Bloomfield, Leiss, *et al., The Control of Local Conflict: A Design Study on Arms Control and Limited War in the Developing Areas,* especially Chapter VIII, prepared by the author.

[21] See the case study of the Philippine insurgency by Col. Thomas L. Fisher II in *The Control of Local Conflict: Case Studies,* Vol. IV, p. 54. (Col. Fisher also acted as director of the project as a whole.)

(but not impossible) that the availability of this class of weapon can be effectively controlled at reasonable cost, or without unrealistic requirements or international cooperation. Insurgents often have difficulties in acquiring adequate stockpiles of weapons and ammunition and often have to pay exorbitant prices for them. Nevertheless, the fact remains that they have, more often than not, been able to obtain what they needed, in spite of occasionally intense and competent efforts to block the flow of arms.

Since World War II, more than 40 countries have manufactured military small arms including pistols, rifles, carbines, submachine guns, and light machine guns. The United States, Soviet Union, and Communist China far outrank the other countries in their scale of production, and furthermore, the enormous transfers of small arms to the developing world—a result of military assistance programs since World War II—have sharply reduced the market for the smaller manufacturers. It is fair to say that military assistance has been responsible for most of the arming, not only of regular armies, but also of their enemies, the insurgents. This is due not only to the frequent capture of weapons from the regular armies, but also—given the unpredictability of political trends in the less developed countries—to the fact that the control of weapons often changes hands in ways that neither the donor nor the original recipient would have considered desirable.[22] For example, when Castro came to power in Cuba in 1959, he acquired control of all the weapons in government arsenals that had been provided by the United States to the Batista regime throughout the 1950's. To these were added the various standard NATO rifles and submachine guns he was able to purchase from Belgium that year. By 1960, however, the Soviet Union had established itself as Cuba's principal donor of military equipment, and then, as the Cuban army standardized on Soviet weapons, the U.S. and NATO equipment was rendered surplus. It should not have been surprising to learn, in 1963, that an arms cache discovered in Venezuela, apparently for use by communist insurgents, consisted of weapons of U.S. and Belgian manufacture. Similarly, weapons supplied by Britain to the Egyptian army prior to the departure of the British Military Mission in 1949 later found their way into the Algerian and Somalian conflicts. One factor tending to reinforce this retransfer potential is the longevity of small arms. In the Cyprus conflict of 1963-1965, some of the Turkish Cypriotes were armed with Mauser bolt-action rifles which the Turkish army had purchased from Germany at the turn of the century. Furthermore, these rifles may well have been smug-

[22] John H. Hoagland, "Arms in the Developing World," *Orbis*, Vol. XII, No. 1, Spring 1968.

gled into Cyprus aboard a submarine provided by the United States to Turkey under a military assistance agreement.[23]

The world inventory of automatic and semi-automatic weapons, which are especially prized by insurgents, may now stand at about 35 million, including the Soviet-designed AK-47 rifles, about an equal number of NATO FN "FAL" rifles, and a somewhat lower number of M-1 Garands and M-1, M-2, or M-3 carbines.[24] There may also still be about 50 million bolt-action rifles in the world inventory, including the Soviet Mosin-Nagant, British Lee Enfield, German Mauser, Japanese Arisaka, and perhaps about 3 million U.S. Springfields.

Of the total world inventory of bolt-action rifles and automatic or semi-automatic weapons, a very rough but reasonable guess of their approximate distribution might be about one-third in the control of each of the two major military alliances and a third everywhere else, largely in the less developed countries. Until the mid-1950's, bolt-action rifles were among the most prevalent military small arms in the less developed countries. Since the later 1950's, shipments of arms to the less developed countries have probably been dominated by semi-automatic and automatic rifles and submachine guns. (In one extreme case, 20,000 M-16 rifles were sold to Singapore before the U.S. and allied requirements had been met in Vietnam.)

Submachine guns, in contrast with rifles, are among the least complicated small arms to manufacture. The parts are more easily fabricated from sheet and light stock and require less precision of manufacture because of the type of action employed. Consequently, a number of countries that are making no other effort to produce rifles or machine guns are engaged independently in the manufacture of submachine guns. Among these are Burma, El Salvador, Iran, Peru, Thailand, and Uruguay.[25]

Generally speaking, there are very few successful designs of military small arms. Those that are successful are then produced under license in various countries. For example, a Belgian light automatic rifle designed for NATO use is manufactured at 13 separate arsenals in 11 countries, all under Belgian license. In addition, the manufacturing cost of small arms is still fairly modest. The average cost of the M-16 automatic rifle to the U.S. government is slightly over $120 per unit, compared with roughly $50 per rifle during World War II. Ammunition for the M-16 costs the U.S. government about $.08 per round.[26]

[23] *Ibid.*
[24] See Hoagland and Clapp, *op. cit.*, pp. 10-21, for all of the figures cited here.
[25] *Ibid.*, p. 16.
[26] *Ibid.*

It does not lie within the scope of this article to deal with the question of arms supplied to the national forces of less developed countries under military assistance agreements.[27] It should be pointed out, however, that the vast majority of weapons entering the developing world have come through this channel, and as some of the previous paragraphs point out, their ultimate disposition is far from certain. Clearly, a great deal of rethinking is now needed and will continue to be needed regarding the role of military assistance and training in the years to come. The Nixon Administration showed its awareness of this problem when it supplied Cambodian forces with captured stocks of communist weapons in the spring of 1970 rather than introducing large numbers of new weapons into the region.

Marshall McLuhan reminds us that Amanullah Khan, the Amir of Afghanistan, said, after firing off the first torpedo supplied to his armed forces: "I feel half an Englishman already."[28] Weapons have a strongly symbolic role, especially the prestige weapons which can be flown or driven in elaborate displays of force on national days of celebration. Experience gained to date indicates with considerable certainty that much of the more sophisticated weaponry has little relevance to the control of insurgency. Aerial bombardment, for example, has seldom been effective against small numbers of insurgents in difficult terrain. In many cases, it has served only to alienate the civilian population against the counter-insurgent force and drive them into supporting the insurgents. A case in point is provided by the Cuban insurgency, in which the Batista government dispatched aircraft to bombard all suspected areas of rebel activity. As a result, pilots dropped explosives and napalm on villages, houses, and crops, raising popular hostility against the regime.[29] Similarly, in Algeria, the French used tactical aircraft to bomb and strafe suspected guerrilla hiding places with the end result of punishing the population rather than hurting the insurgents.[30]

A national air force, faced with an insurgency, might consider itself ill-advised for political reasons to admit openly that its very expensive capabilities were not ideally suited to the threat at hand. Instead, it might be

[27] A major study of arms transfers, with special reference to military assistance and training is presented in Amelia C. Leiss, Geoffrey Kemp, *et al.*, "Arms Transfers to Less Developed Countries," MIT Center for International Studies, Publication C/70-1, February 1970. Also see Geoffrey Kemp's excellent study, "Arms Traffic and Third World Conflicts," *International Conciliation*, No. 577, March 1970.

[28] Marshall McLuhan, *Understanding Media: The Extensions of Man* (New York: McGraw-Hill, 1964), p. 296.

[29] *The Control of Local Conflict: Case Studies*, Vol. II, p. 129.

[30] *Ibid.*, Vol. III, p. 89.

thought preferable in most cases to dispatch sorties and expend a great deal of ordnance against targets that suit the weapons—all in order to be able to report operational activity. The Iraqi air force, in its operations against Kurdish insurgents, is said to have conducted "an indiscriminate and harsh bombing campaign against Kurdish forces. All of these efforts proved unsuccessful and only served to alienate increasingly larger numbers of the population from the government. In the space of three or four months in 1961-62, about 500 villages were bombed and strafed, leaving 80,000 Kurds homeless."[31]

The Changing American View of Insurgency

In the early post-war period, Stalin's offensive in the Eastern Mediterranean, which involved direct and indirect territorial claims in Turkey, Greece, and Iran and an intensive effort to bring down the Greek government in favor of a puppet regime, quickly followed the creation of satellite governments in the Eastern European countries. It was the Greek insurgency, in particular, that led Washington to the formulation of the Truman Doctrine of 1947, which stated that "it must be the policy of the United States to support free peoples who are resisting subjugation by armed minorities or by outside pressures."[32]

One must also keep in mind some of the other elements at work in this period, especially the Chinese Civil War, which by 1949 resulted in the expulsion of Chiang Kai-shek's government from the Mainland. Also by 1948, rebellion had broken out in Malaya and in the Philippines, adding to American concerns that the hard-won victories of World War II might be quickly swept away by a new kind of aggression. All of these, in addition to Korea and the Berlin blockade, created deep and lasting concerns in the west (which are, to some extent, still with us) about Soviet and Chinese grand designs. Thus, the Domino Theory became much more than just a theory. It quickly became a fixed assumption which helped

[31] *The Control of Local Conflict: Case Studies*, Vol. III, p. 180.

[32] President Truman's address to Congress, March 1947. In his memoirs, *Present at the Creation* (New York: W. W. Norton, 1969), Dean Acheson has written (p. 194):

> When the attempt moved beyond the Soviet-occupied areas of Eastern Europe to West Germany, the Balkans, and the Middle East, the United States Government gave fair warning that, if necessary, it was prepared to meet Soviet force with American force, rather than with mere protests and resolutions in the United Nations. The first warning was given in August 1946 but Stalin continued to probe cautiously and to receive firm but cautious responses until June 1950, when throwing off pretense, he made an attack in force through a satellite on the other side of the world in Korea. Here the American response was unequivocal.

dictate the American response to insurgency. Dean Acheson remembers speaking to Congressional leaders, in preparation for massive U.S. military aid to Greece in 1947, along the following lines:

> Like apples in a barrel infected by one rotten one, the corruption of Greece would infect Iran and all to the east. It would also carry infection to Africa through Asia Minor and Egypt, and to Europe through Italy and France, already threatened by the strongest domestic Communist parties in Western Europe. The Soviet Union was playing one of the greatest gambles in history at minimal cost. It did not need to win all the possibilities. Even one or two offered immense gains. We and we alone were in a position to break up the play.[33]

Several years later, in the mid-1950's, President Eisenhower viewed the situation in Southeast Asia in similar terms. As he has written: "... if Indochina fell, not only Thailand but Burma and Malaya would be threatened, with added risks to East Pakistan and South Asia as well as to all Indonesia."[34]

However disreputable the Domino Theory has now become, it was probably a fairly effective operative assumption in the earlier post-war period, instilling in Washington the will to resist and prevent what might otherwise have been a series of comparatively easy communist victories in the Balkans, the Middle East, and Asia. These victories could have isolated large segments of those areas from normal international traffic and commerce. The assumption that the theory was valid for a number of years derives mainly from the fact that successful insurgencies during these years often depended on the willingness of a contiguous state to provide matériel support and sanctuary to the insurgents. Large-scale support by the major communist nations often depended on this condition, without which success was, in the past, much less likely.

Since World War II, it seems clear that there were two peak periods of concern in Washington's perception of the threat of local conflict. The first came in the immediate post-war years, when European governments were trying to reestablish or redefine their colonial relationships and Stalinist Russia was embarked on a series of global thrusts. The second peak period came in the immediate post-Sputnik years (1958 to 1962) when the establishment of new states in Africa and Asia reached its numerical peak, politico-military instabilities were very high, and the Khrushchev regime was at the height of its missile rattling style of diplomacy. In this period,

[33] Acheson, *op. cit.*, p. 219.
[34] Dwight D. Eisenhower, *Mandate for Change* (New York: Signet Books, 1965), p. 404.

Soviet doctrinal support of "wars of liberation" (e.g., in Cuba, the Congo, Vietnam, and Laos) became explicit and appeared to the west to be abnormally dangerous.

Partly as a consequence, few U.S. defense issues received greater attention in the 1960's than counter-insurgency. Starting in 1961, when President Kennedy entered office, American concerns over the apparent success of communist insurgency began to crystallize into a new structuring of American general-purpose forces, especially as part of the new doctrine of flexible response which replaced what was regarded as an inflexible and unworkable doctrine of massive retaliation.[35] The emphasis on counter-insurgency created a new military emphasis on Green Berets, pre-positioning military stockpiles, fast-deployment logistics ships, and massive long-range airlifts, all of which signalled a clear U.S. intention to intervene directly against communist insurgency.[36] The Cuban revolution and the subsequent Bay of Pigs invasion, as well as rising concerns about the course of events in Laos and Vietnam, gave the strongest reinforcement to those who argued in favor of meeting the communist threat precisely at its point of most rapid advancement. It is instructive to review the documents of that period as a reminder of how readily many of those who now condemn the war in Vietnam then accepted the clear and high-minded logic of a U.S. policy of counter-insurgency.

It did not take long, of course, for second thoughts to set in. It seems doubtful, in fact, that President Kennedy ever really placed the unqualified emphasis on counter-insurgency that is credited to him.[37] One of the clearest signs of emerging caution was provided by Defense Secretary Robert McNamara's famous speech at Montreal in May, 1966, in which he said:

> . . . the United States has no mandate from on high to police the world, and no inclination to do so. . . . The plain truth is the day is coming when no single nation, however powerful, can undertake by itself to keep the peace outside its own borders. Regional and international organizations for peacekeeping purposes are as yet rudimentary, but they must grow in experience and be strengthened by deliberate and practical cooperative action.[38]

[35] See, for example, Maxwell Taylor, *The Uncertain Trumpet* (New York: Harper and Brothers, 1959).

[36] At least to this writer, it also seems apparent that UN peacekeeping, foundering in the wake of the Congo operation and the death of Dag Hammarskjold, probably received its *coup de grace* when official Washington headed down the road of flexible response.

[37] See, for example, his second State of the Union message, which points out America's inability to manage the world's revolutionary tides.

[38] *The New York Times*, May. 19, 1966, p. 11.

Read five years later, this statmeent reflects the slowly emerging viewpoint that it was time to review the potential for a truly international security-keeping system in the Third World to augment and slowly supplant the present alliance systems. Although there are many reasons to believe that such an attempt would not have worked (e.g., continuing Soviet opposition, hesitancy in the UN Secretariat, middle-power disenchantment, and disinterest in the less developed countries, to name only a few), it still seems regretable that the United States did not take more positive steps to show its interest in and willingness to pursue this goal.[39]

The American agonies during 1965-1968 can now be discerned as a watershed period in reorienting American attitudes toward security in the Third World. It was a period in which the full potential costs of U.S. intervention were brought home to the American public as they had earlier been demonstrated to the French people both in Vietnam and Algeria. Since 1968, and the advent of a new Administration, the viewpoint has emerged in Washington, further enforced by the events of May 1970, that concomitant with withdrawal from Vietnam, the United States must also limit the kinds of situations which can lead to direct U.S. military involvement in the less developed countries. This viewpoint, enunciated as the Nixon Doctrine, also assumes that American allies in these countries must be encouraged to develop their own capabilities for self-defense and that the United States, for its part, must be prepared to adopt a generous role in providing military assistance. The Nixon Doctrine is more a statement of attitudes befitting the current political climate than a set of operational policies. This is not necessarily a bad thing, given the continuing need for American flexibility in an uncertain world. However severe the trauma of Vietnam may have been, it still seems obvious that the United States, with its diverse private and public interests abroad, will not be able to ignore the issues of military security in the less developed world during the 1970's.

Some Possible Future Trends of U.S. Security Policy in the Third World

"Historically," C.G. Jung writes, "it is chiefly in times of physical, political, economic and spirtual distress that men's eyes turn with anxious hope to the future, and when anticipations, utopias and apocalyptic visions multiply."[40] This observation may help to explain the recent out-

[39] For a detailed discussion of the future potential of UN peacekeeping see *The United States and UN Peacekeeping: A View Toward the 1970's*, a study prepared under the author's direction by Bolt, Beranek and Newman Inc. of Cambridge, Massachusetts, for the Office of the Assistant Secretary of Defense, International Security Affairs (November 1966).

[40] C. G. Jung, *The Undiscovered Self* (Boston: Little, Brown and Co., 1957), p. 11.

pouring of forecasts and predictions of future trends. Here, a few possibilities about the 1970's are suggested in order to assess the validity of some of the now prevailing views about the future U.S. role in the security of the Third World. Taking a very broad look at possible future trends, at least seven different types of military conflict short of general war suggest themselves as possibilities in the 1970's:

1. A continuation of the combined interstate-internal military conflicts in Southeast Asia, with a great deal of external involvement and support;
2. The continuing rise of urban terrorism in Latin America and a corresponding decline of the semi-romantic rural insurgency;
3. The growing importance of interstate conflict in the Middle East, with increased potential for major power confrontation, and a probable relative decline in the importance of insurgency;
4. Potential warfare involving the colonial remnants and racial confrontation in Africa south of the Sahara;
5. The continuing use of terrorism in all its forms by dissident or separatist groups in the advanced industrial societies;
6. Popular reformist uprisings in Eastern Europe, with possible spillovers into the west; and
7. Finally, Korea should continue to be regarded as a very special and very dangerous situation.

This list, to the extent that it is valid, suggests that insurgency *per se*, while still very important, may be a smaller element in the total security environment of the 1970's than it was in the 1960's. Insurgency may be bracketed by interstate war on the one side and low-level violence and terrorism on the other side, interacting with both and standing less often by itself as a source of major policy concern to the United States. Among the most critical determining factors of future trends will be the attitudes and actions of the Soviet Union and Communist China. A few other nations, such as Cuba and North Vietnam, should still be regarded as potential exporters of violence, but they are inherently limited in the scale of their promotional efforts.

The Soviet role in local conflicts will, of course, be a major determinant of American perceptions. One important new trend that became visible in the later 1960's was what appeared to be Moscow's own belated version of Washington's fast-deployment, general-purpose forces of the early 1960's. As Thomas Wolfe has written regarding the emerging Soviet capabilities for military intervention:

> . . . the present regime has moved in this direction building on measures initiated in the Khrushchev era to improve Soviet amphibious and

airlift capabilities, to train the reactivated marine forces (naval infantry) in landing operations, and to secure base arrangements growing out of Soviet military aid programs abroad. The dispatch of Soviet naval units, including special landing vessels, to the Mediterranean in connection with the 1967 Arab-Israeli crisis was a clear example of this trend.[41]

Moscow obviously prefers to support established national governments that are regarded as progressive in socialist terms and that can be expected to provide a generally cooperative environment for Soviet programs abroad. Coincident with this preference has been a continuing sense of caution about providing support directly to anti-government insurgent groups such as Al Fatah. In the post-Khrushchev era, and probably also in the wake of the Congo fiasco, Moscow's rhetoric concerning wars of liberation has toned down considerably.[42] In general, the establishment of relations with friendly regimes, including the acquisition of base rights, will be implemented whenever an opportunity presents itself. This will probably continue to be an important element of Soviet foreign policy in the 1970's, especially in cases where strategically located nations can be weaned away from western ties and influences by means of political and economic aid. This strategy is now reinforced and supported by a token umbrella of Soviet security guarantees based on the new capability to deploy not only general-purpose forces but also strategic systems. (The Allende regime in Chile, for example, combining a constitutional mandate with a Marxist philosophical base, might appear to Moscow to be an ideal candidate for such efforts.) The risk to western interests in all of this is the potential Soviet use of cooperative nations as warehouses, operational bases, or proxies for the further fomenting of conflict and insurgency. This will be covered by a Soviet strategic presence of nuclear submarines and long-range strategic aircraft operating from bases in the Caribbean, Mediterranean, and Indian Ocean.

The Chinese potential for fomenting insurgencies along its territorial borders will remain considerable in the 1970's, even though many China watchers continue to emphasize Peking's innate sense of caution about foreign involvement. However, it seems likely that China may be both willing and able, when specific foreign policy purposes are served, to sup-

[41] Thomas W. Wolfe, "Soviet Military Policy," *Current History*, October 1967, pp. 7-8.

[42] Although, as Joshua and Gibert point out, this terminology does not, in Moscow's view, refer exclusively to insurgencies but to any Third World conflict in which there is a Soviet preference. See Wynfred Joshua and Stephen Gibert, *Arms for the Third World: Soviet Military Aid Diplomacy* (Baltimore: The Johns Hopkins Press, 1969), pp. 113-116.

port insurgency in other Asian nations. Recent efforts in Vietnam, Thailand, and Burma, and future possibilities in all of these areas plus India's northeastern provinces and even Pakistan, support the general expectation that China will occasionally play such a role. The Chinese may also continue to provide long-range support of distant insurgencies, particularly where the Soviet Union is too cautious to act—for example, in support of insurgent groups in Africa and the Middle East. As Chinese shipping construction expands, this capability will grow, but it will still be restricted by domestic priorities and diplomatic isolation in the 1970's and may often create unacceptable risks of international opprobrium to many of the potential recipients. In the main, however, the principal Chinese impact on regional security and insurgency will lie in contiguous areas of Southeast Asia, where a confusing array of insurgencies, combined with incursions by regular forces from proxy states across long and poorly policed borders, will continue to provide tempting opportunities for Chinese advantage. The most severe challenge that this threat presents to Washington is that, as Vietnam demonstrated, it is usually possible to achieve a military standoff in the field but not to obtain a victory in the western sense. Since achievement of the standstill is costly, American popular support is difficult to maintain.

In the wake of the aborted insurgency conducted by Che Guevara and a small band of guerrillas imported into Bolivia in 1967, we may have seen the end, for the time being, of the semi-romantic style of rural guerrilla movements in Latin America. This type of effort, based on Castro's example in the Sierra Maestra and finding its earlier antecedents in the Long March, assumed that a guerrilla force could live and grow among the population, surprise and harass the regular forces, and gradually undermine the authority of the central government until the time arrived for a total seizure of power. In recent years, however, governments have been learning to maintain their composure in the face of this type of threat and to conduct counter-insurgent operations that are well matched to the scope and locale of the insurgency. At least partly in consequence, a new and possibly less threatening type of violence has emerged in urban centers, not only in Latin America but in North America and Western Europe as well.

The Tupamaros in Uruguay are probably among the most ruthless practitioners of urban terrorism, and there are many similar movements in Latin America. Compared with the relatively clear aims of the earlier rural insurgencies patterned along the lines of Mao, Castro, and the F.L.N. in Algeria, it is more difficult to understand where the terrorists believe they are headed and how quickly they expect to get there. The anonymity imposed by terrorist activities is really not conducive to the establishment of a leadership that can become known and admired by the populace or of a clear alternative to the government in power. Furthermore, the operating methods of the urban guerrillas fail to create an image of either benevolence or leadership. Castro, leading his small band in the Sierra Maestra, could present himself, through the foreign press and other media, as a popular and heroic figure. Those who murder, kidnap, rob banks, and plant explosives are in a far less favorable position. It is no wonder that established governments can view them with greater equanimity and tolerate at least some level of violence, even in their capital cities.

The style and trappings of urban terrorism involve bank robberies (as a source of operating funds), kidnapping domestic and foreign officials as a means of political extortion, robbing armories and national arms depots to provide arms, ammunition, and explosives, bombing public buildings, schools, and industrial facilities (usually after a telephone warning permits the evacuation of people), and occasionally murder. The much-publicized airline hijackings of recent years are another major element of the new style. Even in the advanced industrial countries, these activities have become relatively common. They are normally carried out by a new generation of young activists within existing minority groups, which have a sense of grievance against the system and an impatience with or disbelief in due process. Some obvious examples are the Quebec separatists, the Basques, and the religious minority in Northern Ireland. In the less developed countries, the use of the tactics catalogued above may possibly provide a greater potential for escalation or even the political victory of the dissident elements, but it still seems doubtful that this will usually prove to be the case.

In the immediate aftermath of the 1967 War, Israeli commentators were quick and accurate in their predictions of an Arab movement toward guerrilla warfare. The Palestine Liberation Army (PLA), consisting of about 7,000 men stationed mainly in Egypt and Syria, and the larger Al Fatah, many of whom are stationed in Jordan and Lebanon, have been financed by the wealthy oil-producing states such as Saudi Arabia and Kuwait; trained by the more militant states such as Iraq, Egypt, Syria, and possibly other Arab states such as Algeria; and armed with Soviet and possibly Chinese weapons supplied through these states. Other less militant states such as Jordan and Lebanon have, of necessity, permitted operations from their territories. The ostensibly stateless insurgent movement, over whose actions no established government admits jurisdiction, introduced a new and murky element into the Arab-Israeli conflict. The Soviet Union was reportedly wary of supplying arms to the Palestine guerrilla movements, precisely because of the political volatility of the situation.[43] The Chinese, on the other hand, pursuant to an agreement said to have been reached in March 1965, have apparently supplied arms to the Palestine Liberation Organization. Al Fatah has been equipped with Soviet 240mm Katyusha rockets similar to those used by the Viet Cong. The Soviets are said to have denied urgent requests by Al Fatah for anti-aircraft guns.[44]

However important the Arab guerrillas have been or will remain, it seems most likely that the Arab-Israeli conflict will continue to retain a primarily interstate character. The principal reason is the continuing upgrading of Egyptian forces by the Soviet Union, creating the necessity for the Israeli forces to maintain a balance of power. Second, the Israelis have been adamant in their refusal to acknowledge the disclaimers of neighboring states regarding the lack of jurisdiction over the guerrillas, demonstrating their determination to raise any ostensibly irregular or guerrilla action to the level of interstate conflict. Finally, the Arab guerrillas have been such a disturbing influence to their host governments that a considerable amount of friction has developed between the two. Consequently, although the guerrilla movements will probably remain important and may execute some spectacular operations such as the airline hijackings of 1970, their actual achievements will be limited. The real danger in the Middle East will continue to lie in the confrontation of increasingly sophisticated national military forces and, if Soviet actions continue along their present course, of the increasing presence of major power forces in conjunction with local forces.

The reported attack on Conakry in November 1970, allegedly backed by Portuguese military elements, reminds us that Africa, especially in the areas around the Portuguese colonies of Angola, Mozambique, and Portuguese Guinea and among the states bordering Rhodesia, is still one of the potentially most significant areas of conflict during the 1970's. As the U.S. position during the Nigerian civil war indicates, this country has been generally inclined to avoid involvement ever since the Congo crisis of the early 1960's. It seems most likely that, unless U.S. citizens or facilities were directly threatened, e.g., U.S. military facilities in Ethiopia that might be

[43] John K. Cooley, "Soviets Deny Arms to Arab Guerrillas," *The Christian Science Monitor*, 25 January 1969, p. 1.
[44] *Ibid.*

threatened during internal conflict with the Eritrean rebels or during interstate conflict with the Somalis, the United States will show a strong preference to stand aloof from military conflict on the African continent. But that is not the same as saying that conflict should not be expected, on a fairly broad scale, during the decade. The enormous casualties that have been incurred in the internal and essentially racial wars of Chad and the Sudan indicate what can probably be expected in the 1970's. It is most unfortunate that international peacekeeping and mediation agencies have not been able to assist in these situations.

Finally, a few words may be in order about low-level violence in the western industrial countries and the potential for popular uprisings in Eastern Europe during the coming decade even though these topics lie somewhat apart from our subject of insurgencies. The advanced industrial societies of the west, precisely because of their tolerance, are especially susceptible to violent divisions, particularly in the presence of acutely disturbing factors—for example, a severe economic depression. Our challenge is to maintain a sense of perspective about low-level violence. McLuhan identifies one of the difficulties when he writes:

> Our highly literate societies are at a loss as they encounter the new structures of opinion and feeling that result from instant and global information. They are still in the grip of "points of view" and of habits of dealing with things one at a time. Such habits are quite crippling in any electric structure of information movement.[45]

Those who have grown up in the "electric structure of information movement" are more inclined than their predecessors to act on the basis of instincts than logic. Furthermore, their operating styles are quickly transmitted from country to country, by a sort of instant imagery. The similarity of styles in Uruguay, Brazil, Canada, Spain, the United States, Northern Ireland, Germany, and elsewhere is no accident; but it is emphatically not a sign of some new monolith deliberately orchestrating an attack on the world's institutions.

In spite of the west's susceptibility to low-level violence, it seems more likely that the rigid and unyielding regimes of Eastern Europe will, in the end, suffer most from the freedoms and dynamism of the age of instant communication. In fact, one of the most crucial challenges to western policy-makers in the 1970's may be to choose a course of humane response to the revolution of rising expectations in Eastern Europe.

In conclusion, it seems clear that even the agonies of the Vietnam ex-

[45] McLuhan, *op. cit.*, p. 297.

perience will not lead to a full-fledged American retreat from the less developed world and its security affairs. Obviously, the 1970's will have to be a "cool" decade from a policy standpoint. Some low-level violence at home and abroad will have to be treated with great tolerance, but just as obviously, there will be crises in which the outcome matters a great deal to the United States and which will demand an American response. If that were not the case, this country would already have evacuated all of its forces from Vietnam and denied military assistance to Israel and Cambodia, and it would not be seeking to balance Soviet naval power in the Indian Ocean.

Generally, however, we must remind ourselves that a peaceful, non-military environment, characterized by free international trade and transportation, usually favors both the west and the less developed countries and is, in fact, the most revolutionary influence that can be introduced into the developing world—raising expectations, making socio-economic discrepancies more obvious, and creating a turbulence that, however disturbing it may occasionally be, will almost certainly produce beneficial effects over the long term. On the other hand, a militarized environment, for example in the Mediterranean area, generally favors the more militant and less liberal powers because it tends to suppress the free intercourse of trade and transportation among large numbers of states and emphasizes the symetrically arrayed military power of only two very large states—thus perpetuating the myth of a dual Russian-American hegemony. Generally, the Soviet Union lacks a very impressive ability to engage in peaceful trade and commerce, but its strategic and general-purpose deployments abroad seem to be increasingly threatening.[46] Just as generally, the United States finds its main strength on the international scene in the commercial and technological realms. It seems reasonable to suggest that the United States should, in the 1970's, risk presenting a less military face to the developing world. Even in the face of Soviet or Chinese military threats, the U.S. should make even greater efforts than it has in the past to augment the flow of normal trade, tourism, and commerce between the less developed states and the world at large by means of its many available mechanisms of aid, finance, and enterprise.

Washington has clearly recognized the delicate balancing act that will be needed to deal with localized military crises of the 1970's—in par-

[46] For example, the ominous build-up in Cuba, including the facilities at Cienfuegos capable of accommodating nuclear submarines and the numerous visits of TU-95 long-range reconnaissance aircraft. (See *Aviation Week*, December 21, 1970, pp. 16-17.)

ticular, the need to keep a lower profile without abandoning whole segments of the world's population to regressive influences. One hopes that, despite the Administration's apparent disenchantment with the efforts of civilian defense planners and the "think tanks" that assist them, some capability, greater than what now exists, will be rebuilt to deal with the complexities of the Nixon Doctrine in a period of continuing tension.